YORK NOTES

WITHDRAWN

DEATH OF A SALESMAN

ARTHUR MILLER

NOTES BY ADRIAN PAGE

 Longman

 York Press

We are grateful to Rogers, Coleridge & White Ltd in association with Internationl Creative
Management on behalf of Arthur Miller for permission to reproduce extracts from *Death of a
Salesman*, Copyright © 1948, 1949, 1951, 1952 by Arthur Miller, Renewed 1975, 1976, 1979, 1980.

YORK PRESS
322 Old Brompton Road, London SW5 9JH

PEARSON EDUCATION LIMITED
Edinburgh Gate, Harlow,
Essex CM20 2JE, United Kingdom
Associated companies, branches and representatives throughout the world

© Librairie du Liban *Publishers* 1998, 2003

First published 1998
This new and fully revised edition first published 2003
Second impression 2004

10 9 8 7 6 5 4 3 2

ISBN 0-582-78425-5

Designed by Michelle Cannatella
Typeset by Pantek Arts Ltd, Maidstone, Kent
Produced by Pearson Education Asia Limited, Hong Kong

CONTENTS

PART ONE
INTRODUCTION

How to study a play 5

Reading *Death of a Salesman* 6

PART TWO
THE TEXT

Synopsis 8

Act I 10

Act II... 24

Requiem 41

Extended commentaries

Text 1 – Telling Willy the news (Act II, pages 84–5)...... 43

Text 2 – Playing your hand (Act I, pages 34–9) 46

Text 3 – Asking the boss a favour (Act II, pages 59–64) 54

PART THREE
CRITICAL APPROACHES

Characterisation

Willy 62

Biff and Happy.. 67

Linda 71

Ben 74

Bernard 75

Charley 76

Howard Wagner 78

The woman 78

The two girls 79

Theatrical techniques

Realism 80

Expressionism 81

Staging 82

Montage 83

Structure 84

Themes

    Capitalism and the value of life 84

    An ordinary man 86

Language and style 88

Signs and symbols 88

PART FOUR
CRITICAL HISTORY

Tragedy? 90

Heroic status 92

Social drama 94

Man in society 96

Politics 97

Psychoanalysis 98

The family 98

Gender 99

PART FIVE
BACKGROUND

Arthur Miller 101

    His other works 102

Historical background 102

    Capitalism 103

    The American Dream 104

    McCarthyism 105

Literary background 105

Chronology 108

FURTHER READING.. 110

LITERARY TERMS 114

AUTHOR OF THESE NOTES.. 115

PART ONE

INTRODUCTION

HOW TO STUDY A PLAY

Studying on your own requires self-discipline and a carefully thought-out work plan in order to be effective.

- Drama is a special kind of writing (the technical term is 'genre') because it needs a performance in the theatre to arrive at a full interpretation of its meaning. Try to imagine that you are a member of the audience when reading the play. Think about how it could be presented on the stage, not just about the words on the page.

- Drama is always about conflict of some sort (which may be below the surface). Identify the conflicts in the play and you will be close to identifying the large ideas or themes which bind all the parts together.

- Make careful notes on themes, character, plot and any sub-plots of the play.

- Why do you like or dislike the characters in the play? How do your feelings towards them develop and change?

- Playwrights find non-realistic ways of allowing an audience to see into the minds and motives of their characters, for example soliloquy, aside or music. Consider how such dramatic devices are used in the play you are studying.

- Think of the playwright writing the play. Why were these particular arrangements of events, characters and speeches chosen?

- Cite exact sources for all quotations, whether from the text itself or from critical commentaries. Wherever possible find your own examples from the play to back up your opinions.

- Always express your ideas in your own words.

These York Notes offer an introduction to *Death of a Salesman* and cannot substitute for close reading of the text and the study of secondary sources.

CHECK THE BOOK

Ronald Hayman's book *How to Read a Play* (revised and updated 1999) is an excellent introduction to the study of drama.

READING *DEATH OF A SALESMAN*

Reading a play is not like reading a novel; the words alone do not convey all the meaning. For example, when in the Requiem, Happy says, 'I'm gonna win it for him [Willy]' (p. 111), Biff directs a hopeless glance at him. This wordless expression is vital to our understanding, since it reveals the fact that Biff is able to detect the mistake that Willy made and to see it being perpetuated by Happy. By this time Biff is beyond argument. The glance shows how much he has learnt. In reading a play, it is essential to try to create the scene you are reading in your own mind, so that you are able to imagine a performance on stage. Arthur Miller's stage directions are there to help actors and readers realise the play in this way.

CHECK THE BOOK

Martin Esslin discusses the role of stage directions or the *Nebentext* in *The Field of Drama: How the Signs of Drama Can Create Meaning on Stage and Screen* (1987).

Readers also need to ponder the exact implications of every statement in the play: Arthur Miller's characters do not always mean what they say or say what they mean. When in Act I Willy says that he is 'not dressing to advantage' (p. 29) and that people have begun to laugh at him, Linda replies:

> Willy, darling, you're the handsomest man in the world –
> WILLY: Oh, no, Linda.
> LINDA: To me you are. [*Slight pause.*] The handsomest.
> [*From the darkness is heard the laughter of a woman.*]

Here we can guess Linda's thoughts and motives. Her first statement that Willy is the most handsome man in the world is pure exaggeration, and Willy is not comforted by it. Linda then corrects herself and adds that he is the most handsome man *to her*. This is as good as withdrawing the compliment, however, since it will not make Willy feel that he is appreciated at work. Linda appears to realise this, and adds, 'The handsomest', as if to compensate for her blunder. She is choosing her words carefully to reassure Willy and support his ego. The laughter of another woman (that only Willy and the audience can hear) adds another dimension. Willy's memories – about which we are to learn more as the play progresses – cut against Linda's attempts to console him.

Readers should not overlook the stage directions, as these also contain vital information, and are often just as significant as the dialogue. We should try to work out how the stage directions add to our understanding before proceeding to the next piece of dialogue. For example, in the scene above, Linda takes off Willy's shoes. This shows that Willy is, indeed, exhausted, and it also demonstrates the extent of Linda's commitment to him. He accepts the gesture without thanking her or showing any surprise. Some women might find this demeaning, but we learn something about Linda and about Willy from this piece of stage business.

Some aspects of the text are, and will always remain, ambiguous. It is best to describe this ambiguity rather than trying to solve it, since ambiguity is part of the text's richness. To continue with the example above, does Willy's refusal to acknowledge Linda's kindness signal a lack of care, or total exhaustion? Or both?

> LINDA: You don't talk too much, you're just lively.
>
> WILLY [*smiling*]: Well, I figure, what the hell, life is short, a couple of jokes. [*To himself*] I joke too much! [*The smile goes.*] (p. 28)

Willy here seems to enjoy Linda's appreciation of his humour. It is his humour that attracts the woman in the hotel to have an affair with him, and Willy responds quickly to flattery. The smiling seems to signify this. His public face and his private face are directly contrasted here. To his wife, he defends his light-heartedness; whereas in secret, he knows that he overdoes the humour. This is an example of Willy's self-knowledge and contradictions.

As Arthur Miller himself says: '*Death of a Salesman* is a slippery play to categorize because nobody in it stops to make a speech objectively stating the great issues which I believe it embodies' (Introduction to *Collected Plays*, reprinted in *Plays: One*, Methuen, 1998, p. 32). For this reason, every speech should be considered in the light of the character's personality and function in the play. It is the whole play that expresses Arthur Miller's vision of society and the nature of individuality: no single character acts as his mouthpiece, nor does any single speech offer an unmediated statement of his views.

CONTEXT

It took Arthur Miller six weeks to write the finished script of *Death of a Salesman*.

PART TWO

THE TEXT

Page numbers refer to the latest Penguin Twentieth-Century Classics edition throughout.

SYNOPSIS

 CHECK THE NET

See http://www.ibiblio.org/miller/ for more information on the play and the playwright. This is the Arthur Miller Society official site; it has links to other sites related to Miller and his contemporaries.

Willy Loman, an ageing salesman with two grown-up sons, Biff and Happy, has reached the point where he is so tired he can no longer travel to sell his goods by car. The play follows the last twenty-four hours of his life. His sons are concerned about his mental state, but his wife is always supportive. Willy's thoughts are shown to us in a number of dreamlike scenes from the past which are enacted during the play's course. Willy has always focused his hopes on Biff and he has coached him to be a sports star and to follow in his father's footsteps by using his charm like a salesman. He is very unhappy that Biff has a manual job on a farm and he argues with Biff about his future career. Biff is insecure and anxious to improve himself and to 'get on'. Act I ends on an optimistic note as Happy comes up with the idea that he and Biff will sell sports goods and organise basketball demonstrations to promote them. Willy and Linda also think this is a 'one-million-dollar idea' (p. 50), and Biff promises to visit his former employer, Bill Oliver, to ask for a loan to start the business. Willy has always been very proud of Biff's sporting skills and has despised other boys such as Bernard who have been more academic. This scheme, if successful, will enable Biff to make something of himself and Willy to see his hopes for the family's financial security come true at last. Willy decides at the same time to ask his boss, Howard, to allow him to work in New York rather than travelling by car to distant locations.

At the beginning of Act II, Willy is refused a non-travelling job and Howard asks him to stop working altogether. There are more and more daydreams where Willy relives past glories with Biff on the sports field and discusses the route to success with his now dead brother, Ben. Ben is held up as an ideal by Willy since he fulfilled the American Dream of starting out with nothing and becoming rich by effort. Charley, a neighbour, offers Willy a job, but it is refused.

An ordinary job would not fulfil the great expectations Willy has of himself and Biff. Willy goes to meet Biff and Happy in the restaurant where their celebration is planned, but the boys are trying to seduce two young women. Biff has failed to reach any kind of deal with Bill Oliver and has, in fact, run out of the building having stolen his fountain pen. Biff begins to realise that he is chasing a form of career success which will not really make him happy. He also realises that his past has been made to seem more glamorous than it really was. Willy demands to know how the meeting with Bill Oliver went and is furious when he is told that no deal was concluded. He desperately needs good news. Eventually the boys seek to rebuild his optimism as he becomes increasingly distressed. Willy's mind then drifts back to incidents in the past, including the moment when Biff discovered him in a hotel room with another woman.

The boys leave Willy in the restaurant, and when they return home their mother is outraged that they have abandoned their father. Willy, meanwhile, has bought some seeds and is trying to sow them in the garden at night. This is a bizarre attempt to fulfil a long-held ambition to leave something behind him that will grow. This leads to a family row. Biff has decided that he is to blame for his own lack of success, and tries to leave the family home for good, but Willy accuses him of attempting to hurt him. In frustration, Biff declares that no one in the house has ever told the truth for ten minutes. He shows Willy the gas piping which his father had concealed so that he could commit suicide. Biff also reveals that he has been in prison for theft and informs Willy that his dream of having a son who will achieve greatness is not going to happen. Biff's love for his father becomes apparent, however, and in a final gesture of love for his son, Willy commits suicide in order that the family can at least collect the twenty thousand dollars' insurance.

CHECK THE BOOK

See C. W. E. Bigsby's book *File on Miller* (1987) for a slightly longer synopsis of the play.

ACT I

The play is not divided into conventional scenes, although there are recognised points at which the action changes significantly. These divisions are not made explicit because the play is intended to be as 'seamless' as possible in the **realist** tradition. To make these summaries easier to follow, the two acts are divided into numbered sections which follow the changes of action and location.

SECTION 1 (pages 7–13)

- Willy Loman's sales career is coming to an end.
- Willy is exhausted, and wants his son Biff to be successful.

Willy Loman returns to the family home in Brooklyn, showing signs of great weariness, and his wife's greeting indicates that she is concerned about him. Willy's reply, 'It's all right. I came back' (p. 8), tells us immediately that the possibility of a dangerous accident has been on both their minds. It also suggests that Willy might have been contemplating not returning. The music of the flute which is heard during this scene adds a note of sadness. Willy has been driving home from Yonkers to Brooklyn, where he lives, at the rate of ten miles an hour because he is unable to concentrate on driving safely. At first he blames the car and Linda accepts this, but he eventually admits that it was his driving which was at fault. He has been asked to sell goods in distant parts of America, instead of New York, and he is deeply exhausted by the travelling. Willy believes that if the original boss of his company were still alive, he would be in charge of the New York area by now. This is the first of many speculations by Willy about what might have been in different circumstances. He blames the boss's son, Howard Wagner, for his lack of career success. Willy believes that his relationship with Howard's father was much better and would have earned him promotion. Linda, Willy's wife, is very understanding and comforts Willy. He is about to go out to send a wire to his colleagues when she takes off the jacket he has put on, indicating that she wants him to relax. Willy seems to pay little attention to this consideration, but agrees to her suggestions. He tells Linda that she is 'my foundation and my support' (p. 13). We learn from the stage directions that Linda loves Willy for the big dreams he has and endures all his petty cruelties.

Biff and Happy, Willy's two sons, have been out on a date together with two women, and Linda tells Willy how much she enjoys the atmosphere they create in the house. Willy, however, is depressed at the thought that although he will soon own his house, there will be no one to live in it as his two sons are grown men. There is a difference between Linda's acceptance of loss such as children growing up, and Willy's feelings of dissatisfaction. He feels that some people 'accomplish something' in life (p. 10). (What other differences are there between Linda and Willy? What similarities are there? Is Linda the perfect wife? Is she to blame for allowing him to behave like this?)

Willy is unhappy that Biff appears not to have accomplished anything because he is not earning very much money by working on a farm. Biff has been very upset by Willy's attitude towards him. Willy cannot simply accept things as they are. His life seems to lack fulfilment. He decides to help Biff to get a profitable job, as if he can find fulfilment through his sons' successes. This is one of those moments in the play where Willy makes a decision to change his ways. Willy reflects on Biff's popularity and attractiveness as a young man with obvious pleasure. He begins a long period of thinking of the boys' childhood and how Biff used to polish the family car very well. This seems a very insignificant virtue to admire in a son. Linda says that 'life is a casting off' (p. 10), but Willy is unable to let the past go. Linda's behaviour calms him down and he agrees to be less severe with Biff.

COMMENTARY

Willy's mental state is exhibited in this first scene and we are presented with a number of possibilities. Is he going mad, or is he merely very tired? There could be several explanations for his behaviour. Later on he kills himself deliberately whilst driving. Is this an attempt to prepare his wife for his death by telling her how badly he has driven on the way home? Arthur Miller began the writing of the play with Willy's first line in his mind, and its ambiguity helped him to develop the character of Willy. Is Willy

> **CONTEXT**
>
> Willy is angry because 'In the greatest country in the world a young man with such – personal attractiveness, gets lost' (p. 11). This echoes the Calvinist doctrine that some people are given gifts by God and it is morally wrong not to use their talents.

explaining that he is home early or reassuring a wife who believes that one day he will not come home at all?

The arch supports in his shoes and his wife's motherly attention to him combine to give a rather pathetic picture of an old man. On the other hand, his determination to go out and sell to Brown and Morrison, together with his anger, makes him a more admirable figure. His decision to seek a non-travelling job may seem brave, as he appears resolved to control his life. He at least has the energy to resist his fate. When Willy attacks the way in which the greenery in his neighbourhood has been removed by building work, he seems a sympathetic figure. At this point he talks rationally about a familiar problem of modern life. This introduction to Willy enables the performer to emphasise the contradictory aspects of his character. Linda's statement that he makes 'mountains out of molehills' (p. 13) also poses a fundamental question. Is Willy inventing his own difficulties, or is he the victim of a terrible fate? Who or what is the cause of his unusual behaviour?

CONTEXT

Making mountains out of molehills means making small problems seem much greater than they are.

Section 2 (pages 14–21)

- While their father rambles, the sons discuss their sense of personal failure and their ambitions.

As Willy is daydreaming about the past, his sons, Biff and Happy, are waking, and on stage they can be seen to overhear the conversation between Willy and Linda from their bedroom. They too are aware of Willy's increasing forgetfulness and poor attention. They speculate as to whether their father is colour-blind, which adds further to the growing sense that Willy lives in a world of his own making, which is distorted. While the boys talk, Willy is seen muttering to himself, which reinforces their comments about him.

Biff says, 'I'm like a boy' (p. 17). Their conversations about women are openly sexist and indicate a lack of maturity. Happy refers to one woman with whom he had his first sexual encounter as a 'pig' (p. 15). This, however, is a play which was written before the upsurge of interest in sexual politics, and such attitudes in 1949 would have been more prevalent than they are now. This is not to say that the attitudes expressed by the boys are condoned by the play. Such behaviour is not a source of happiness. Biff enjoys the freedom of farm work, but feels that he should be 'makin' my future' (p. 17). Happy points out that he now lacks confidence and Biff immediately refers to his father's criticisms of him. (Is Willy responsible for his sons' lack of achievement?)

Happy has a good job, a flat, a car and lots of girlfriends, but he too is dissatisfied and 'lonely' (p. 17). Neither man is married. They each appear to envy the other's way of living. Happy would love to show off his physical prowess in the store by, for example, outfighting the others. The competition for job success is transformed into a competition for the more physical pleasure of sexual success. Happy explains that he views women as conquests, and takes pleasure in seducing colleagues' women for sport. He enjoys ruining or sleeping with the girls who are involved with his senior colleagues and attending their weddings out of a sense of competition, but he hates himself for these compulsive acts of cruelty because he is fundamentally honest. Sexism, therefore, is not something that brings happiness or a sense of triumph. (What other sexist attitudes are there? Are they also shown in a negative light?)

Biff imagines that if he could buy a ranch he could combine commercial success with his love of the outdoors and its physicality. Biff decides to contact Bill Oliver to ask for sponsorship. He used to work for Bill Oliver but was dismissed when he stole a carton of basketballs. At this stage the boys are optimistic that they can work together to achieve what they both want. They are both worried about their father, whose mutterings on stage while they talk justify their concern.

COMMENTARY

Biff and Happy discuss how unusual Willy's behaviour is, and they are deeply concerned about him. The sons' voices on stage may seem like a running commentary on their father as he speaks to himself downstairs. It appears at first as if Willy's worries about Biff's future are the cause of his talking to himself. Willy clearly idealises Biff and also attacks him cruelly for his lack of career success. He can only think of Biff's ability to polish the car with pride. By implication, Biff does not have a great deal to be proud

> **CONTEXT**
>
> Biff's worry that he is 'wasting' his life because he earns so little echoes the Protestant ethic which sustains capitalism. The biblical injunction to make the most of your talents means that moral value is measured by economic success.

> **CONTEXT**
>
> Happy is anxious that he is not acquiring capital by buying a house like his marketing manager.

> **CONTEXT**
>
> Happy's worry about ruining women refers to the moral attitude dating from the nineteenth century, when a woman who had had sex might never get married because of her reputation.

about. Biff hints that his father has other worries besides him. Biff's worries about 'not gettin' anywhere' (p. 16) are an echo of his father's worries about his job. (Will the sons end up like their father? Can they detect his mistakes and put them right? Are they about to make the mistakes which condemned Willy to failure?)

Biff's enjoyment of farm work echoes Willy's love for the grass and trees which he misses. Happy's desire to take off his shirt and live a more natural life also sounds rather similar to this. Happy has compromised and taken an ordinary white-collar job, but Biff has refused to compromise. He prefers the farm life without a career. Neither man is happy, however. This is emphasised in their relationships with women. Biff does not have a relationship and Happy's are shallow. This is not, however, because they are unattractive. They too are dissatisfied like their father. Biff is uncertain whether he should aim for career success and where he can find fulfilment. Happy is concerned at his lack of any real moral feeling for women.

Section 3 (pages 21–9)

- Willy is lost in daydreams about family life when his sons were young.

The stage lighting changes, and music also alters the mood as we now see Willy in the kitchen. Willy is lost in a dream of the past. This is emphasised by the stage direction that the characters enter through the walls, making the transparent divisions on stage seem even more dreamlike. This section is like a flashback in a film as Willy recalls his conversations with the young Biff when he was waxing the car. Willy condones the theft of a football on the grounds that Biff is well liked and no one will object. Through the flashback, we can compare Willy's hopes for the future with what we know from the beginning he has achieved. Willy tells the boys: 'Someday I'll have my own business, and I'll never have to leave home any more' (p. 23). This is clearly one of those resolutions that Willy fails to achieve. Willy proudly proclaims that he is liked wherever he sells and tells his sons that this is very important. Biff is a successful football player, and Willy makes fun of Bernard, a

GLOSSARY

Gene Tunney a famous American boxer

Jumping rope (US) skipping rope

open sesame the phrase that opened the robbers' cave in the tale of Ali Baba in *The Thousand and One Nights*

knickers knickerbockers, loose-fitting knee-length trousers gathered at the knee on a band

Regents a state exam which is marked externally

sneakers trainers

graduate him grant him a diploma allowing him to go on to university

Adonises in Greek mythology Adonis was a beautiful young man loved by Aphrodite

What do we owe? the Lomans have purchased items such as the refrigerator and vacuum cleaner on hire-purchase, meaning that they have to pay for them in regular instalments

scrim a curtain of heavy cotton fabric

younger boy who reminds Biff of the need to study for his maths exam. Popularity appears more important to Willy and he makes a connection between being popular and being successful.

Willy boasts that he has sold a great deal on his latest trip, but is forced to admit to Linda that he has exaggerated. When the calculations are done, the family is desperately short of money. Willy admits that 'the trouble is, Linda, people don't seem to take to me' (p. 28). Once again, we see that Willy is pretending to himself and others that he is successful and popular. Linda kindly consoles Willy as he expresses self-doubt about his appearance and his abilities. He thinks that people laugh at him. As she lovingly tells him that he is the most handsome man in the world – to her – a woman's laughter is heard. The other woman's laughter suggests possibilities to the audience. Is it true that people do laugh at Willy, or is the laughter directed at Linda for being so naive? The laughter may signify that the woman understands how Linda is trying to support Willy's confidence by telling him the things he wants to hear. In this case the woman is sharing with Linda a joke about how credulous men are and how easily they are flattered. Hearing the woman's laughter so soon after this exchange between husband and wife makes us think about what has been said.

COMMENTARY

Willy has been daydreaming about the past and Biff's youth, and now the past begins to dominate his consciousness. From now on, Willy has increasing difficulty in distinguishing the past from the present. In his idyllic dream, he and Biff enjoy the two elm trees which the builders have now taken away. This adds to the feeling that he is losing his mind. The performer can signify this by his attitude as he looks directly towards the wall and acts as if he can see things.

The dream of his sons' youth and their physical beauty allows Willy to relive his past triumphs when he could congratulate himself on the boys' talents. Now his daydreams are enacted on stage as if they were really happening. The past is taking hold. Increasingly he imagines things the way he wants them to be rather than the way they are.

QUESTION Should we feel sympathy for Willy or despise him for his lack of faithfulness? Is it possible to have both these attitudes at once?

CHECK THE BOOK As Willy reveals the workings of his mind he shows that **Expressionist** drama 'was the dramatization of the subconscious, a kind of scripted dream'. See J. L. Styan, *Modern Drama in Theory and Practice: Expressionism and Epic Theatre*, vol. 3 (1981).

Willy's belief that his sons' popularity will enable them to succeed in business can be seen as an answer to the previous scene. Willy believed that they would succeed because they were 'liked' when they were young.

Willy's boastfulness, however, is undermined by the fact that he has not earned enough money to pay the bills. He begins to question whether he is, in fact, as popular as he claims.

SECTION 4 (pages 29–31)

- Willy remembers his lover in Boston.

Willy continues as if he is speaking to Linda, but the woman takes up the conversation and it gradually becomes clear that she is his lover. The stage is lit in such a way that the woman can suddenly appear to Willy and they can be alone together as if they were in the hotel room in Boston where they made love. He explains how loneliness on the road and self-doubts have plagued him. The woman pays him compliments and likes him because he is amusing, a 'kidder' (p. 30). The running together of the tender scene of married life and the affair shows Willy to be insincere and guilty. As he expresses his love for his understanding wife, a flashback recalls the affair. The woman thanks Willy for a gift of stockings and comments that she has lots.

As the memory of the woman in the Boston hotel room fades, the scene returns to the kitchen of Willy's house in Brooklyn. Linda is mending old stockings and continues to console Willy by telling him that he is handsome. Willy tells her to throw out the stockings, but Linda puts them in her pocket, presumably to resume the mending later.

CONTEXT

The gift of stockings is particularly generous, since stockings were in very short supply during the war years and were highly valued by women.

COMMENTARY

Following the scene where Willy admits that 'people don't seem to take to me' (p. 28) comes the memory of the woman he had an affair with – someone who did like him, who claims to have 'picked' him (p. 29). On stage now, the lighting is focused on this woman and Willy, so that he enters fully into this imagined moment. This is the first reminiscence which has changed the location from the Lomans' house. Up until this point, Willy's daydreams have compensated for the harsh reality in which he is living by reminding him of more optimistic moments. Like Happy, he feels guilt because of his success with women.

Setting the scene of Willy and his lover in the middle of the scene between Willy and Linda exposes Willy's lack of integrity. He cannot remain faithful to the one person who is completely faithful to him. Willy gives stockings to his mistress, hence his guilt when he finds Linda mending her stockings – the implication is that he has indulged his lover at the expense of his wife.

Section 5 (pages 31–2)

- Willy remembers Biff's failure at school.

Young Bernard bursts on stage to inform Willy that Biff will fail maths. Linda joins in the criticisms of Biff by adding that he treats the girls roughly. Willy is assailed by a number of memories which show that Biff was not such a perfect young man. In despair, Willy simply defends his son instinctively. Linda cries because she cannot make an impression on Willy. Night falls and Willy seems to be '*wilting*' (p. 31).

COMMENTARY

The recollection of scenes from the past is not always idyllic. This is more of a nightmare, which comes swiftly on the heels of the guilt caused by the affair. Willy's memory of Biff is marred by the thought of his petty thefts and his failure to study maths successfully when he was training for sport.

The Regents is a maths exam which, like A levels, is marked externally. To assist Biff in this exam would be a crime. Willy, however, has no compunction about asking Bernard to help Biff. Willy clearly encouraged Biff to become a sportsman to make him proud, and Biff suffered as a result. Willy, however, shrinks from accepting this thought.

QUESTION
Does Willy demand that Linda throw out the stockings because he is unable to live with the guilt associated with them, or because he does not want to see his wife wearing mended stockings which make her look poor and, by implication, make Willy look unsuccessful?

Willy gets angry when Biff is criticised and defends him with the words: 'He's got spirit, personality' (p. 31). Willy is oblivious to the fact that he might have encouraged Biff to steal, and he maintains that he only told him to do decent things. Self-deception is a prominent feature of Willy's character.

SECTION 6 (pages 32–4)

- Willy daydreams of the life he might have led if he had worked with his brother, Ben.
- Charley comes in and he and Willy begin to play cards.

Willy laments the fact that he did not go to Alaska like his late brother Ben, who fulfilled the American Dream by starting out with nothing and becoming rich in diamond mines. Willy refuses financial help from Happy and from Charley, a successful neighbour. Charley's offer of a job is rejected, apparently out of pride. Willy is proud of his ability to work with his hands and resorts to this when he has nothing else to be proud of. Handling tools is identified with masculinity.

COMMENTARY

Willy's memories are extending further and further into the past. He now goes back to a much earlier incident when he might have made his fortune. Talking to his son Happy, Willy says, 'The world is an oyster, but you don't crack it open on a mattress' (p. 32). The phrase means that you have to work to succeed, but also implies that going to bed with people is not a means to economic and social success. Willy is able to make perceptive remarks, but is not always able to follow his own advice.

QUESTION
How many of Willy's problems are the result of his views about what makes a man?

A note of despair enters when Willy says: 'The woods are burning' (p. 32). This poetic metaphor recalls both the elm trees which Willy loved and the jungle where Ben made his fortune. The implication seems to be that the very land of opportunity itself is going up in smoke. This scene reveals some of Willy's qualities which he ignores. He is a skilled craftsman, and Charley respects this, but Willy regards it as natural in a man.

SECTION 7 (pages 34–41)

- Willy plays cards with Charley, but conducts a conversation with his dead brother, Ben.
- Charley leaves, and Ben talks of his success.

As Willy plays cards with Charley, Ben, Willy's dead brother, enters. The entrance in most productions will be made through the supposed walls, to show that this is an unreal event as the playwright directed. Willy confuses Charley with Ben, and a dialogue with the dead brother follows. Ben was the only man who ever 'knew the answers' (p. 35), according to Willy. Charley leaves, unhappy with Willy's strange responses and inability to concentrate on the card game. Willy's replies to his dead brother begin to be confused with his conversation with Charley.

Ben enters into conversation with Willy and Linda as if he had returned and was alive. Willy asks Ben: 'How did you do it?' (p. 36). Ben speaks of their father, who, it turns out, played the flute. The flute at the beginning of the play now seems to recall this fact and imply that the spirit of Willy's father is somehow present. More flute music is heard, although this is on a lighter note and celebrates the dead father. Willy encourages Biff to pretend to box with Ben, but Ben tricks him and throws him down. He warns Biff never to fight fair with a stranger.

Inspired by Ben, Willy suddenly decides to do some building work on his property and sends the boys off to steal some material from a nearby building site. Willy is not worried when Biff is chased by the watchman, and refuses to believe that he is stealing anything. Ben and Willy collude in encouraging hearty, 'manly' behaviour in the boys. Charley and his son are despised because they 'can't hammer a nail' (p. 40). Willy pleads with Ben to stay a few days because he did not know his father well and, as he says, he feels 'kind of temporary about myself' (p. 40). This is a very revealing remark and tells us that Willy is not sure of himself and feels constantly that he is about to change in some manner. Ben, however, is determined to leave for a business appointment and they stand at opposite sides of the stage as they say goodbye. This is a sign that they are opposites and their attitudes are completely different. When Ben first enters, the stage direction says he is *utterly certain of his destiny* (p. 34), unlike Willy. (What other differences are there between the two men?)

Ben's account of how he made his fortune is straightforward: 'William, when I walked into the jungle, I was seventeen. When I walked out I was twenty-one. And, by God, I was rich!' (pp. 40–1). Despite the differences between the two brothers, Willy concludes that Ben's message is the same as the one he has preached to his sons.

COMMENTARY

For the first time, Willy is unable to distinguish what is going on about him from the imaginary visit of his brother. Ben is an imagined rather than a remembered character. It appears that he is a figment of Willy's imagination whose purpose is to reinforce Willy's ideas. The audience, however, may interpret Ben differently. He can be made to sound arrogant and scathing about Willy's lifestyle. Willy's attempts to impress him can seem embarrassingly naive. It is clear that Willy suffers from a lack of self-understanding and he turns to Ben as a substitute father figure. Ben does not tell him the secret of success, however. He repeats the formula 'when I walked into the jungle, I was seventeen', and this can be taken to mean that there is no answer. In this episode, Willy seems to make Ben mean what he would like him to mean. The disparity between the reality which the audience can perceive and that which Willy can see is greater than ever.

> **CONTEXT**
>
> Henry David Thoreau, the American philosopher, attacked the idea of making quick fortunes through gambles such as Ben's diamond mines. Thoreau thought it contradicted the Protestant spirit of honest toil.

SECTION 8 (pages 41–54)

- Willy's plans to commit suicide have been discovered.
- Linda defends her husband.
- The Loman family decides on a business plan.

The section begins as Linda enters to find Willy still musing on his conversation with Ben. Linda tells Biff that Willy is always excited when he is coming home and then becomes increasingly tense when he actually arrives, as if he 'can't bring himself to – to open up to you' (p. 42). Linda will not allow Biff to criticise his father and she explains that she will not allow anyone to make Willy depressed. To Linda, he is 'the dearest man in the world' (p. 43). Biff attacks his father, and argues that Charley would not express himself so violently, 'spewing out that vomit from his mind' (p. 44). Linda defends Willy stoutly, and argues that he must not be allowed to die without dignity. She excuses his strange behaviour by asserting that he is simply exhausted. In addition, he has been put on 'straight commission' rather than earning a fixed wage. This means that he is earning a great deal less. 'Attention, attention must be finally paid to such a person', argues Linda (p. 44).

In saying this, Linda is suggesting that Willy is a potentially tragic figure. He too can be reduced to bad behaviour by circumstances beyond his control. Willy may not have achieved a great deal, as she points out, but he did have high ideals which he has been unable to realise: 'he's a human being, and a terrible thing is happening to him … A small man can be just as exhausted as a great man' (p. 44). The difficulties that Willy has been facing begin to dawn on the boys and Linda delivers a forceful speech which details Willy's sales career and its attendant troubles:

> And what goes through a man's mind, driving seven hundred miles home without having earned a cent? Why shouldn't he talk to himself? Why? When he has to go to Charley and borrow fifty dollars a week and pretend to me that it's his pay? How long can that go on? How long? You see what I'm sitting here and waiting for? And you tell me he has no character? The man who never worked a day but for your benefit? When does he get the medal for that? Is this his reward – to turn around at the age of sixty-three and find his sons, who he loved better than his life, one a philandering bum – (p. 45)

A question which is frequently posed in some form is whether Willy is a tragic figure as Linda suggests here. Is Willy to blame for his present situation or has he been the victim of circumstances which he could not control?

GLOSSARY

salary … straight commission Willy is no longer paid a monthly wage; he now earns money only when he sells something, when he receives a percentage of the sale

stake give financial support to

They broke the mould when they made her there is no one else like her; no one else matches up to her

Hercules in Greek mythology a hero famous for his strength

CONTEXT

The reference to 'great' men recalls Aristotle's view of tragedy that it only happens to important people who can fall from a great height. In this play tragedy extends to ordinary men.

Biff agrees to stay in the house and get a job, but he reminds his mother that Willy threw him out of the house because he knows that his father is 'a fake' (p. 45). Biff does not explain at this stage, but is on his way upstairs when his mother tells the sons that their father is trying to kill himself. His car 'accidents' have been deliberate and a woman witness has seen him deliberately crashing into a bridge. Linda has also found a length of piping which can be attached to the gas and used to commit suicide. Linda hides the pipe during the day but replaces it when Willy comes home so that he does not know that it has been discovered. She feels that he lived his life for the boys and that they have turned their backs on him. Linda tells Biff that his father's life is in his hands (p. 47). (Is it true that the sons have been responsible for Willy's behaviour or is Linda exaggerating?) Biff apologises and promises to reform.

Happy and Biff are having a heated dispute about Biff's attitude to work when Willy returns. Happy accuses Biff of behaving foolishly by whistling in the lift when he was employed. Biff wishes he were a carpenter who would be allowed to whistle. As Willy enters he joins the conversation immediately and tells Biff that he never grew up. Biff is also compared unfavourably with Bernard, who now has a serious job in business and would not whistle. This is in stark contrast to the scenes when the boys were young and Willy made fun of Bernard. Biff retaliates by playfully accusing Willy of also whistling in the lift and this sends Willy into a rage. He is calmed, however, when he hears of Biff's idea to consult Bill Oliver about sponsorship for a business selling sports goods, but he dismisses the idea when he learns that it is only a plan. Willy and his sons begin to imagine how they could all start a business selling basketball gear and the whole family becomes excited at the prospect. Willy's annoyance with Biff is not due to a lack of faith in him. He tells Biff that he has 'a greatness' in him (p. 53).

 QUESTION
Does Willy accuse Biff of the faults which he hates most in himself, or is Biff guilty of idleness?

Willy starts to give Biff advice on how to approach the meeting about sponsorship: 'Everybody likes a kidder, but nobody lends him money' (p. 51). Perhaps Willy is trying to advise Biff not to copy his own errors. Happy and Biff begin to plan and Happy tells Biff that he will be able to get any 'babe' he wants once he is successful. Once again, sexual success and commercial success are treated as if they were the same. Willy, however, cannot resist overstating his advice, and he eventually offends Biff. He reminds him of the theft he committed long ago and tells him not to do it again. At the very end of Act I, Willy comes to the front of the stage and loses himself in a memory of Biff's sporting achievements on the American football field when he was a schoolboy. The golden glow in which Biff is bathed suggests that he is being idealised and that the vision of what Biff can achieve is unrealistic.

Linda is still puzzled by Biff's remark about Willy being 'a fake' (p. 45) and asks Willy what Biff has against him, but Willy says he is too tired to continue. The final sequence of events needs to be examined carefully. As Linda is preparing to go to bed, the light of the gas fire becomes noticeable and Biff stares at it. Willy promises Linda that he will ask Howard, his boss, to let him work in New York and reassures her, but then Biff finds the piping behind the heater and looks towards his parents' bedroom. This suggests that Willy is a genuine suicide risk as Linda has claimed. Biff takes the piping away, wrapped around his hand, as Willy admires the moon. Willy's final poetic reference to the moon indicates that this scene concludes optimistically with the family united in the desire to see Biff succeed.

> **? QUESTION**
> Is the description of Willy as 'a fake' an accurate description of his behaviour throughout the play?

COMMENTARY

The sons are by now very worried about Willy's mental state as he continues to proclaim that Ben was right. He is retreating into his own world. His memory is also suspect as he fails to recall that he pawned the one valuable gift which Ben gave him.

Biff begins to attack his father, but Linda's speech in Willy's defence is memorable and persuasive. It can make Willy seem like a dignified victim. Linda blames Biff for his father's condition, but Biff cannot reveal his father's affair. This is what makes Willy 'a fake'. When Willy's suicide plans are discovered, the 'solution' which creates domestic harmony is for Biff to start a business. This will please Willy, appease Linda and restore Biff's self-confidence. Biff is acting for the sake of other people, however, and not himself.

The petty argument about whistling exposes rifts in the family which are difficult to heal. Biff makes a number of altruistic concessions, but Willy again attacks him when he comes home.

CHECK THE NET

http://research.
haifa.ac.il/~theatre/
amiller.html has a
list of all Miller's
major works with
brief synopses, as
well as links to
other Miller sites.

The accusation that Biff never grew up is cruel in these
circumstances. Willy is again boastful and calls himself 'Big shot'
(p. 48). The attempt by Biff to redress the years of failure is
ignored and he is still criticised. It is especially cruel of Willy to
compare Biff to Bernard and to argue that he does not whistle in
lifts. In earlier days, Willy mocked Bernard and encouraged Biff to
do so as well.

Despite the way he is treated, Biff does take responsibility for his
father when he removes the rubber piping so that he cannot commit
suicide. Biff is trying hard to be the model son after all these years.

ACT II

SECTION 1 (pages 55–9)

- Willy decides to ask for a non-travelling job.
- Meanwhile Happy and Biff are planning a meal in a restaurant
  to mark the launch of the business.

The music which begins Act II is cheerful and reminds us that the
Lomans are in an optimistic mood as they contemplate a new
business which will make them all happy and might solve all their
problems. Willy has slept in, and is in his shirtsleeves, which
suggests that he is relaxed. Willy decides to buy seeds on the way
home and daydreams again. This time he imagines the family on a
small farm in the country. (It is ironic that Willy should idealise
this kind of life while he condemns Biff for working on a farm.)
Willy is confident that he will be able to convince his boss to
relocate him in New York. Financial worries still trouble Linda,
however, and she also asks Willy to request an advance payment so
they can meet their bills. The one good point is that they are about
to make the final payment on their mortgage so that they will own
their house outright. Linda sends Willy off to see Howard. She has
a stocking in her hand, and Willy asks her to put it away, reminding
us of his affair and his guilt. This occurs just as Linda is taking
great care of him and reminding him of all that he needs to take.

Biff and Happy have arranged to meet their father for a celebratory meal at six o'clock, and Linda mediates between the boys and Willy. She asks them to be kind towards him and to remember that he is 'a little boat looking for a harbour' (p. 59). This sentimental expression shows how she cares for Willy while also recognising his weaknesses.

COMMENTARY

Willy has slept well, apparently because he can now imagine a happy future for the family. He is confident and determined to insist on a non-travelling job.

His angry denunciation of consumer society seems rational and justifiable. Linda, however, shows us how misleading this appearance is as she follows him around with a mended jacket. Despite his bold manner, her act of buttoning his jacket makes him seem less in control of things.

Willy's claim that he is going to 'knock Howard for a loop' (p. 57) harks back to the aggressive masculinity which he instilled in his sons. The salesman's approach to such a meeting is to prepare himself psychologically as if the correct mental attitude will win the day. Critics have noted how the salesman's philosophy of life is one by which Willy lives. But can the right mental attitude change the job market?

SECTION 2 (pages 59–66)

- Willy fails to persuade his boss to give him a non-travelling job despite a desperate emotional plea.

The stage lighting is dimmed on Linda, and Howard Wagner comes on stage where he is brightly lit. We are now in Howard's office in New York. Willy's arrival is barely acknowledged by Howard as he enters, since Howard is adjusting a tape recorder. This is in contrast to Willy's claims that people are usually delighted to greet him. It is some time before Howard can stop demonstrating his new machine. Howard is unable to think of a sales position for Willy in New

GLOSSARY

wire-recording machine a tape recorder

Jack Benny's programme a US comedian, Jack Benny (1894–1974) hosted long-running shows on radio and TV. *The Jack Benny Show*, a radio programme, began in 1932 and was heard every week for twenty-three years

York. Willy begins to make emotional appeals to Howard, and reminds him that he was the person who agreed with his father that he should be called Howard. Despite this emotional pressure, Howard simply does not have a position to offer Willy. Howard does not appreciate Willy's approach to the situation. When Willy launches into a long story about his past, the actor playing Howard must make this lack of sympathy clear.

Willy explains that when he was a young man, he refused the chance to go to Alaska where gold had been discovered because he was convinced that selling was the career for him. He cites the example of an elderly salesman called Dave Singleman who inspired him by selling successfully in his eighties.

Here Willy reveals the source of the hold which selling has on him. He cannot imagine a more wonderful end to a long career than being able to phone twenty or thirty different cities and be remembered and loved as a salesman. Willy is especially moved by the number of colleagues who attended Dave's funeral. What Willy appears to need more than anything is to be liked and admired. This speech may be acted with great force, but it can also be seen as a rather pathetic sentiment. Willy laments the passing of the days when personality counted and the profit motive did not dominate selling. (What evidence is there that Willy is well liked? Is he deluding himself completely?)

CONTEXT
Willy's high sales in 1928 were made during the period of economic boom which preceded the Depression in America.

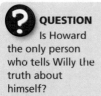

QUESTION
Is Howard the only person who tells Willy the truth about himself?

Willy becomes increasingly desperate and almost begs Howard to give him a job. As Willy lowers the weekly wage he would settle for, so Howard becomes even more resolute and refuses. Willy resorts to reminding Howard of one of his most successful years when he sold well, but Howard insists that he is exaggerating. Willy suddenly realises that he is shouting at his boss and begins a dialogue with Howard's father. As he addresses an empty chair as if it contained the late Frank, Willy suddenly switches the tape on by mistake and we hear the voices of Howard's children. The surprise causes Willy to shout out, and reveals how disturbed his mental state is. He begs Howard to shut the machine off. Howard is aware that Willy has 'cracked up' before and he now tells Willy that he can no longer work for the company. He advises Willy to seek the help of his sons. Howard understands that Willy is indulging in 'false pride' (p. 65) when he tells him that his sons are involved in a big deal.

COMMENTARY

Howard must be played in such a way that he sees through Willy's behaviour and refuses to be moved by his rhetoric. The conversation shows that economic facts cannot be changed by emotion. The belief on which a salesman's life is founded – that his psychological approach can win the day – is shown to be a myth. There are possibly echoes of the 1930s Depression: a man cannot conjure up a job, however good he is. In desperation Willy asks to be sent to Boston where his lover promised he would be passed straight through to the buyers, but even this doesn't work.

SECTION 3 (pages 66–70)

- Willy dreams of the old days when Biff was a sporting success.
- The figure of his late brother, however, reminds Willy that he has nothing to show for his life so far.

Howard exits, wheeling off the recording machine, and Ben enters to the music which has become associated with him. Willy's mind is now switching in confusion between past and present. Ben offers him an opportunity in Alaska, but Linda is cross about this and rebukes him. She asks why everybody feels they must 'conquer the world' (p. 67). She argues that Willy has a good job and is well liked, hence it would not be advisable to move. The family is a factor that prevents Willy from becoming too adventurous in his choice of career. Willy and Linda claim that he is 'building something' with this firm, but Ben asks: 'What are you building? Lay your hand on it. Where is it?' (p. 67). Willy is fond of building and has put in a great deal of work on the porch. He is good with his hands, but this symbolises the only thing which he has built: his house. This is all he has to show for his sales career.

Despite the fact that Willy is deceiving himself, his view that a man needs to feel that he leaves something behind must not be discounted. Money alone does not motivate him. The American Dream suggests the pioneers' ambition to settle down and build their own home as well as venturing out into the wilderness and making their fortune. Willy is torn between these two impulses but decides that he is 'gonna do it here' (p. 68). When Willy begins to extol the virtues of Dave Singleman again, prompted by Linda, Ben leaves rather than listen. This suggests that Willy is a bore.

As if to restore his morale, Willy now turns his attention to Biff dressed as a high-school boy with Happy carrying his American football kit. This is a flashback within a dream. This is Willy's retort to Ben's offer of another job. He argues that the whole wealth of Alaska passes over the table at the Commodore Hotel. In other words, footballers who win can make more money than Ben in Alaska. He states that the wonder of America is that 'a man can end with diamonds here on the basis of being liked!' (p. 68). Willy is sure that when Biff goes into business, doors will open for him because he is liked. Willy recalls Biff's football game at Ebbets Field and how ecstatic he was at the prospect. Charley nearly drives Willy to violence by making fun of the game and Willy's attitude. Willy challenges Charley to a fist fight because he mocks the game.

COMMENTARY

When Ben asks Willy if he wants to work in Alaska, he uses masculine imagery to emphasise the mental attitude needed to triumph: 'Screw on your fists and you can fight for a fortune up there' (p. 66). It appeals to Willy at first, but Linda rejects the idea. She does so because she has believed Willy's claims that he is making a career with his firm. She appears to have swallowed his rhetoric wholesale. Linda's attitude, however, is opposed to this male adventuring, and there is something of a clash of ideologies here. Linda is emphasising the virtues of domestic stability as opposed to seeking one's fortune. It is interesting to note that Willy is trapped by his own boasting. He cannot contradict what Linda is saying without revealing that he was exaggerating. Willy's attitude towards Charley turns violent as he defends his lifestyle and dogmatic beliefs.

CONTEXT

Willy's admiration here for 'the wonder of this country, that a man can end with diamonds here on the basis of being liked!' (p. 68) seems to confuse the American Dream of universal opportunity with sporting success and popularity.

GLOSSARY

carte blanche complete freedom of action

J. P. Morgan John Pierpont Morgan (1837–1913), a famous US financier

---

SECTION 4 (pages 70–8)

- Biff's less 'masculine' schoolfriend, Bernard, has turned out to be very successful.
- Willy is reduced to begging money from Bernard's father, Charley.

The scene immediately shifts to Charley's office. It is particularly difficult for Willy to confront Charley and to beg for money when he has just been so aggressive towards him. The grown-up Bernard is sitting in the reception room of his father's office and his signs of social success include tennis rackets beside his overnight bag. Charley's secretary, Jenny, enters and asks Bernard to see Willy, who is making a commotion outside.

On entering the office, Willy is surprised to see Bernard and congratulates him on his career and his marriage. In many ways Bernard is now what Willy wanted his sons to be: successful, married, athletic. Though anxious to preserve the pretence that his sons are equally successful, Willy asks Bernard confidentially to tell him the secret of success. Bernard agrees to speak honestly about Biff's failings and points out that Biff failed at school in maths because he simply did not turn up to take the exam again. Willy claims he ordered Biff to go to summer school, but he would not. Bernard tells Willy that Biff lost motivation after a trip to Boston to visit his father. As a sign of his desire to give up education, he burnt his prized university trainers in the furnace in the basement. As his close friend, Bernard remonstrated with him, and they had a fight which upset them both. Willy is deeply disturbed by this revelation and responds angrily. He feels that Biff's problems are being blamed on him. Bernard and Willy agree that it is better to persevere in life: 'You know, "If at first you don't succeed … "' (p. 75), but Bernard adds that sometimes it is more sensible to walk away from challenges. Willy suggests that this is what he is incapable of doing. Bernard is leaving to plead a case before the Supreme Court, the highest court in the land.

Charley gives Willy fifty dollars, and Willy has to ask for more to pay his domestic bills, now that he is unemployed. Charley cannot understand why Willy does not accept his offer of a job and feels 'insulted', but Willy says that he 'can't' work for Charley (p. 77). Charley gives Willy the extra money he needs and Willy leaves with a sad farewell, contemplating the fact that he is worth more dead than alive. By now, he is feeling close to Charley, his 'only friend' as he calls him.

> **CONTEXT**
>
> Willy's retort to Bernard – 'If a boy lays down is that my fault?' (p. 74) – is a political question about Liberalism. The play has been accused of uncertainty as to whether each person has ultimate responsibility for his or her actions.

COMMENTARY

As Bernard reveals more and more of his successful lifestyle, Willy begins to lie about Biff. He tells Bernard that Bill Oliver 'Called him in from the West. Long distance, *carte blanche*, special deliveries' (p. 72). He must know this is not true. Willy is unable to sustain his pretence, however, and breaks down when he asks Bernard for 'the secret', completely undermining his boastful attitude. Willy appears not to understand Biff's emotional reaction after the discovery of his affair, but he does ask if he was to blame. This implies that he is deluded rather than uncaring. The very mention of Biff's visit to Boston, however, angers Willy; the audience has started to wonder exactly what happened then. Willy is unable to face the truth about Boston. His apparent sincerity with Bernard has become touching, but his denial of the Boston incident is not honourable.

SECTION 5 (pages 78–87)

- In the restaurant, Biff tries to tell his father that he has not been able to borrow the money from Bill Oliver to start the business.
- Willy finds this news difficult to accept.
- Willy tells his sons he has just been fired.

The scene is blacked out in most productions. We move to the restaurant where Biff, Happy and Willy have agreed to meet up following their business meetings. Stanley, the waiter, and Happy chat and Happy expresses the optimism felt earlier about the day's business. As they talk, a young woman, Miss Forsythe, enters and sits at another table. Happy is attracted to the woman and makes a vulgar remark about her. He asks Stanley to wait on her so that he can begin to talk to her and introduce himself. Happy's rehearsed chat-up lines are recognisably insincere. He tells the woman that she should be on a magazine cover. Miss Forsythe's claim to have featured on many such covers also seems to be implausible and it is likely that they are both lying to impress.

When Biff enters the restaurant, Happy tells Miss Forsythe that his brother is a professional footballer with the New York Giants.

Happy is willing to pass the woman on to Biff, but he lacks confidence. Biff is more concerned about his father. Biff tells his brother that after waiting all day to see Bill Oliver, he realises that he was deceiving himself to think that he had ever been a salesman at the company. He was only a shipping clerk. Biff is beginning to exhibit some of his father's characteristics. (Do you detect any others?) In a confused mental state, Biff has taken a fountain pen belonging to Bill Oliver and run away with it. Happy wants him to please their father by telling him that he has been successful, but Biff is not the kind of person to whom money is lent. He is a thief.

Willy, however, believes in Biff to such an extent that he feels that Biff is deliberately hurting him by not making a success of his life. There is a cruel twist here for Biff. His father depends on him because Willy has failed in his own life. Willy's hopes are pinned on Biff, and Biff is under great pressure to succeed in pleasing the father he loves. Biff feels, however, that he is doomed to failure by his nature. Happy's solution is to give Willy something to live for by lying about a future business meeting with Bill Oliver: 'Dad is never so happy as when he's looking forward to something!' (p. 83).

Biff wants to unburden himself to his father when he arrives, and he begins to tell Willy that he has come to understand his situation better. Biff says, 'I had an experience today' (p. 83). Happy encourages Biff to put an optimistic gloss on the day's events. Just as Biff manages to insist that his father should understand the truth that he never was a salesman for Bill Oliver, Willy tells his sons that he has been fired. At this point, it becomes even more difficult to tell Willy the truth. He demands some good news to tell their mother. Biff is more interested in the fact that his father has been sacked, and Willy persists in asking about the meeting with Bill Oliver. It is Happy who supplies the information that reassures Willy – he implies that Oliver gave Biff a warm welcome and encourages his father to believe that his dreams have come true. A strange conversation ensues with Biff attempting to tell his father the truth about his visit to Bill Oliver's company and Willy demanding to be given good news. Eventually Biff states to Happy: 'I can't talk to him!' (p. 86). At this point there is a single trumpet note which *'jars the ear'*. This is a theatrical way of showing that there is an irreconcilable difference between father and son.

CONTEXT

Biff's assessment of himself can be seen as a curative process, whereby he comes to know himself and thereby shed his neuroses. The play can be seen as an example of Freudian therapy for Biff.

COMMENTARY

When Biff refuses to play the game of telling Miss Forsythe lies in the restaurant, he is experiencing a revelation about himself. Happy is thriving on telling lies like Willy, but Biff has discovered that he has lived a lie for many years. Happy says that 'Selling is selling' or that talking to women is like a business transaction. Biff now wants to face the truth. He deceived himself into thinking that he was a salesman (like his father) but he no longer wishes to propagate lies. He is refusing the 'dream' which his father is living in. Willy cannot accept Biff's 'facts'.

SECTION 6 (page 87)

- Willy daydreams of the time when Biff failed his maths exam.

At this point the lighting on stage changes to allow us to see a scene from the past when Biff's failure in his maths exam was announced to the family. Significantly, this scene is played with young Bernard on stage to remind us that Biff has had very little success in comparison with him. The insertion of this scene, which is usually played on stage behind the restaurant scene, is to show us how Biff's failure to secure the deal with Bill Oliver is just one in a long list of disasters for the family. It is as if we can see what is happening in Willy's mind. In between the playing of the scene where young Bernard tells Linda that the teacher, Mr Birnbaum, has failed Biff at maths, we hear Biff trying to tell Willy about the visit to Bill Oliver. This appears to be the first time that Biff has confronted Willy with the truth about himself.

COMMENTARY

In this scene there is a clue to the way that Willy's mind works, but it is open to interpretation. Does he imagine the occasion when Bernard warned him that Biff would fail maths because he was guilty? Has he worked out the effect that his words had on his son? Can he really face this guilt or does he only face its image?

SECTION 7 (pages 87–91)

- Willy becomes convinced that Biff has failed to negotiate the deal with Bill Oliver to hurt him, and this leads to a violent argument between father and son.
- The memory of the incident when he was in the hotel room with his lover haunts Willy during this scene.

When Biff has finished telling Willy that he failed with Bill Oliver, Willy blames this on his failure in maths. Biff has been brandishing a gold fountain pen and Willy notices the pen and assumes that he has taken this from Bill Oliver. This realisation prompts a memory from the past to haunt Willy as he hears the tannoy system in the Standish Arms hotel. He shouts, 'I'm not in my room!' (p. 87), and the boys realise that he is in a very distressed state. His words no longer seem appropriate to the conversation. Willy is now convinced that Biff is worthless, but Biff in desperation begins to take back what he has said and insists that Bill Oliver has agreed to his business plan and is merely haggling over the amount. Willy seizes on this statement and leaps to the assumption that the deal is finalised, and Biff hastily adds that further meetings are necessary and that he has the opportunity to make a good impression as his father wanted. He is now following Happy's advice to give Willy something to look forward to, but he is also trying not to tell a direct lie. He tells Willy that he cannot go tomorrow. Willy asks him to return the fountain pen, but Biff does not want to add to his problems after having stolen the basketballs. To return the pen now would only confirm him as a thief. Facing Bill Oliver again was an ordeal for Biff, since he would be remembered as a thief from long ago.

Willy does not seem to realise that Biff's motive in going back to Bill Oliver was to please him. In response to Willy's question as to why he went, Biff replies, 'Look at what's become of you!' (p. 89) and we hear a woman's laughter. (What does this laugh mean? Is it a reminder of the days when women admired Willy and he was something, or is it a sardonic judgement on his cruel nature?) Willy becomes angry, hits Biff and concludes that Biff is 'spiting' him by not entering into a deal with Bill Oliver. Willy is clearly unable to understand what Biff is attempting to communicate to him.

> **? QUESTION**
> Is it unkind of Willy to blame Biff when he has put so much pressure on him?

The reason why Willy feels that Biff may be deliberately hurting him seems to lie in Biff's discovery of Willy's adultery. The next scene re-enacts this moment and suggests that it is connected in Willy's mind with Biff's apparent refusal to return to Bill Oliver. Willy and Biff become involved in a physical struggle which is only ended when the girl who featured earlier, together with a companion, returns to the table. During this episode we hear the woman say, 'Someone's at the door, Willy!' (p. 89). Past and present are again confused. Willy talks about opening the door, and he means the hotel door in Boston all those years ago, but he corrects himself and pretends he means the restaurant washroom. Biff tells the girls that his dad is 'A fine, troubled prince' (p. 90), yet Happy denies that he is his father and calls him 'just a guy' (p. 91). Biff is deeply upset by his father's condition. He puts the piping he has discovered on the table and tells Happy that their father is going to use it to kill himself. Happy, however, rejects Biff's argument that he should help their father and is more interested in going out with the girls.

CHECK THE FILM
In the 1985 film directed by Volker Schlöndorff, a much clearer comparison emerges between the sons' sexual appetites and Willy's unfaithfulness, as the two scenes are put side by side.

COMMENTARY

There is almost a biblical feel to this scene as Happy denies that Willy is his father. It is reminiscent of Peter denying Jesus in the Bible. This is a trial of faith, and Happy fails. In a way, Willy is a Christlike figure, who gives his life for others, but it would be wrong to see him only as a holy person.

The scene also shows how impossible it is to break into another person's dream and force them to see the truth. Biff cannot communicate with Willy, and their only course of action is to resort to violence, a typically masculine response. Willy's mind keeps returning to the hotel room in Boston and he is struggling to connect that incident with what is happening now. His defensive conclusion is that Biff is getting his own back. This tells us more about Willy's guilt, however. Sexual desire seems to make all the men in the play feel guilty.

SECTION 8 (pages 91–5)

- The full recollection of the scene in the hotel where Biff discovers Willy and his lover.

Willy and the woman are together in the Boston hotel room getting dressed. The accompanying music indicates that there is passion between them. This a re-enactment of the adulterous relationship Willy had many years ago. The woman is laughing, which reminds us of the laughter we have heard before. Someone is knocking at the door, but Willy is reluctant to answer. The woman comments ironically that Willy has 'ruined' her (p. 92). The same word was used by Happy in Act I (p. 19) when he referred to ruining young women by seducing them. The woman mocks Willy as 'self-centred'. The knocking continues and the couple become increasingly tense as the woman insists that the door should be opened. Willy eventually agrees, after making several excuses, but asks her to hide in the bathroom.

The person at the door is Biff, who has come to tell his father about his failure in maths and to ask him to plead with his teacher to pass him. The maths class came before sports practice and Biff therefore missed it. Willy agrees to speak to Biff's teacher. Just as he is telling Biff to tell the desk clerk that he will be leaving, however, Biff's tale of imitating his teacher and alienating him causes Willy to laugh and the woman joins in. At this point Biff understands that there is someone else in the room. The woman's laugh has acted throughout as a sign of impending disaster and it tends to occur almost as a warning of deception and disgrace. Willy pretends that the woman has taken a shower in his room because hers is broken, and ushers her out. The woman protests and Biff slowly sits down on his suitcase as they argue. The slow motion indicates that he has gathered what is going on. When the woman demands the stockings which Willy has promised her, the nature of the relationship is clear. Biff begins to cry and Willy's pretence fails. Biff now knows that his father is unfaithful. He had imagined that his father was a man of great status and that Mr Birnbaum, his teacher, would listen to him, but now he has lost his regard for him, and his hopes of passing maths have been shattered. He calls his father a 'phony little fake!' (p. 95). Willy tries desperately to explain things to Biff, but Biff is inconsolable. It is particularly saddening to Biff that Willy has given the woman his mother's stockings which she badly needs. Biff leaves and Willy is left on his knees, distraught and shouting at him to come back.

CONTEXT
In some American states at this time adultery was illegal, and Willy gives this as an excuse to make the woman conceal herself.

COMMENTARY

The woman's laugh echoes throughout the play and each time it has a different meaning. At first it is associated with people laughing at Willy, but it turns into an appreciative laugh from his lover. Now it seems to mean callous indifference to the feelings of others. The woman is indifferent to Biff and does not notice what is happening between father and son. Even when he is discovered in the act of adultery, however, Willy seems to ignore reality. He tells Biff not to upset himself and says that he will see his teacher, as if the boy is disturbed by his performance in maths and not by his father's behaviour. This scene makes it clear that Biff's adult life has been a reaction against his father and his father's actions.

> **CONTEXT**
>
> Reacting against one's father is a typically Freudian characteristic.

SECTION 9 (page 96)

- Willy is left alone in the restaurant and becomes disturbed.

The scene in the restaurant is resumed and the kneeling Willy is now consoled by Stanley the waiter. He has been deserted by his sons, who have left with the two women despite having promised to have dinner with their father. Willy is now only concerned about buying seeds to plant.

COMMENTARY

Seeds are symbolic of investment for the future and the farming communities of rural America. The symbol encapsulates all that Willy has wished for.

SECTION 10 (pages 97–9)

- When the sons return home, Linda is furious and tells them to leave the house.
- The boys discover their father planting seeds in the garden at night.

Biff and Happy return home having been drinking. As Happy enters the house carrying a bunch of roses, he looks around for his mother and does not see her. Linda, however, is on stage and rises from her chair where she is sitting holding Willy's coat. She '*rises ominously*' and frightens Happy. Linda is furious that the boys have abandoned their father when he was promised an evening with them in the restaurant. She dashes the flowers to the floor when Happy tells her that they met two girls. Biff pleads with her to see Willy, but Linda is determined to throw the boys out of the house. She tells them to pick up the flowers. Biff does so whilst Happy turns his back on his mother. Happy seems to be oblivious to the hurt he may have caused and Biff grows increasingly angry with him. Biff appears to accept the accusations which his mother is making and begins to express contempt for his own actions in abandoning his father. A hammering is heard and Linda reveals that Willy is planting seeds outside in the dark garden. This strange behaviour causes concern and Biff goes outside despite Linda's pleas not to.

COMMENTARY

Any suggestion that Linda is a drudge who willingly accepts any conditions is dispelled here. She shows real spirit and strength as she chastises the two boys. Her demonstration of her independence also makes us question her relationship with Willy. If she can be so strong, her love for him is freely chosen, and not an indication that she is too weak to do anything else.

QUESTION
Is Linda overprotective towards Willy and blind to his faults?

SECTION 11 (pages 99–101)

- Willy in his disturbed state discusses the pros and cons of his suicide with his late brother as he plants seeds.

The lighting reveals Willy in the darkened garden with a torch, reading the instructions on the seed packets and babbling incoherently. He is still, amongst other things, talking to his brother, who appears on stage. Willy is now considering the prospect of committing suicide and leaving his wife the twenty thousand dollars which his life insurance policy will bring. This seems to be the only way in which he can 'add up to something' (p. 99). Ben, his dead brother, debates the idea with him. Ben points out that the policy

CONTEXT

The cash till **metaphor** in the phrase 'ringing up a zero' suggests that Willy measures his success in life in purely economic terms.

might not be honoured, but Willy feels that the insurance company is morally obliged to do so. The alternative, as Willy puts it, is 'ringing up a zero' (p. 100) at the end of one's life. Ben concedes that the money is a tangible benefit. (Who is right here?) Willy becomes very enthusiastic about the prospect of his death, which he sees as something that can be realised, unlike the promises and hopes he has lived on all his life. He imagines that his funeral will be a spectacular event that will confirm his popularity. He also imagines that this will change Biff's vision of him. Ben believes that Biff will regard suicide as an act of cowardice and hate Willy for it.

COMMENTARY

Willy takes up the conversation with Ben, who has just entered, as if he has been talking to him all along. This is another insight into the state of Willy's mind. Willy has no one to talk to: he has isolated himself in his fantasies. Willy again insists to Ben that he is 'known' (p. 100), despite earlier doubts. Does he have the ability to *make* himself believe what he is saying? Willy is planting seeds in a garden where nothing will grow, and this action undermines the talk of leaving behind something that will survive.

CONTEXT

The planting of seeds on barren ground recalls the biblical parable of the sower and the seed.

SECTION 12 (pages 101–9)

- Biff tries to console his father, who continues to accuse him of spite.
- In retaliation, Biff insists that he face the truth that neither of them is going to fulfil the great dreams Willy has for them.
- Biff does acknowledge that he has always loved his father, however, and this comes as a surprise.
- Willy kills himself to leave the insurance money for Biff.

Biff comes into view in the garden and speaks to Willy. He has come to say a final goodbye. Biff wishes to make his final departure a peaceful one and tries to persuade Willy to come inside to Linda. He repeats that he has come to an understanding of himself, but that he has been unable to communicate it to Willy. He no longer wishes to discuss who is to blame. Biff now sees that nothing will change and that there is nothing anyone can do. He now accepts that he is 'a bum' (p. 102). Biff believes that leaving is now the best thing he can do so that he will be off Willy's mind. Willy can start 'brightening up again' (p. 102). Willy, however, is still obsessed with the meeting with Bill Oliver and refuses to believe that it is not going to take place. He continues to interpret Biff's wanting to leave as 'spite', a deliberate desire to hurt him. Willy refuses to take the blame for Biff's fate, but Biff has been trying to tell him that he has accepted responsibility for his own actions. Willy has been accusing Biff of 'trying to put a knife in' him (p. 103), but it is Willy who has planned his own death.

In exasperation, Biff finally slams the rubber tube that Willy was going to use to kill himself on the table, calling him a 'phony' (p. 103). Biff now tells his father that there will be no pity for him. He also decides that they must both face the full truth. Biff reveals that he has served a prison sentence for theft and that he has been a habitual criminal. He grew up with the impression that he had to succeed within a short period or fail because his father had made him believe that he should be someone important. He describes a revelation that came to him as he ran away with Bill Oliver's gold pen: he suddenly realised that he was happy in the world outside offices where he could relax and be in touch with natural things. Begging for a job suddenly seemed unnatural, a hangover from his upbringing, rather than something springing from his own beliefs.

As Biff tries to make Willy face him, he turns away. Willy retaliates with contradictory hatred: 'The door of your life is wide open!' (p. 105). This statement would normally be a way of indicating the promise and opportunity lying before someone and would be spoken optimistically, but here it is spoken '*threateningly*' (p. 105), according to the playwright's directions. Somehow, America, the land of opportunity, has formed the prospect of endless opportunity into a burden for people like Biff who cannot take advantage of it, yet are expected to by others. Biff has come to terms with his own ordinariness and insists that both he and his father are ordinary people with no great distinction. This infuriates Willy, who has always believed that both he and his sons were destined for great things. There is almost a fight between Biff and his father. Biff tells his father that he should no longer expect him to bring home any prizes.

 CHECK THE BOOK

In *A Critical Introduction to American Twentieth-Century Drama*, vol. 3 (1985), C. W. E. Bigsby discusses the psychoanalytic theory that understanding oneself like Biff is therapeutic.

At this point in the play it would appear that the high expectations that Willy has always had for Biff are the chief cause of their unhappiness. When he finds that he is still unable to communicate the truth to Willy that they are both 'a dime a dozen' (p. 105), Biff eventually breaks down and sobs. Father and son hold each other and find a physical means of expressing their fundamental feelings. Willy cannot understand why Biff is crying and Biff asks him to discard his 'phony dream' before something happens. Willy is deeply moved to discover that, as his wife and Happy tell him, Biff has always loved him. His response, however, shows that he has not absorbed Biff's message when he says that 'that boy is going to be magnificent!' (p. 106).

As Willy says this, Ben appears in the light outside the kitchen. Ben now engages in a dialogue with Willy. In Willy's mind, Ben is confirming his thoughts that the twenty thousand dollars that Biff will have if Willy dies will make him achieve his potential at last. Ben states that it 'does take a great kind of a man to crack the jungle' (p. 106). This implies that perhaps Willy will be a great man if he allows Biff to succeed by bringing the diamond of success out of the darkness of the jungle. Ben's music is now played with dread. Death is the way to bring forth fulfilment for Willy. This is the only way in which he can imitate Ben's career. Willy has turned Ben's recipe for success into his own plan, which involves his suicide. Happy begins again to make the hollow promises of reform that he believes will comfort Willy. Linda now believes that family separation will be the best thing, but when Willy echoes this thought with three words: 'the best thing', Ben also repeats the phrase. This indicates that Willy is not listening to Linda, but is really thinking of his own best plan, which is to die. Left alone, Willy shows his amazement at the revelation that Biff has always loved him.

? QUESTION
Did Willy feel that he had to *earn* Biff's love?

Willy now sees his greatest ambition – success for Biff and himself – about to be realised. Linda entreats Willy to come to bed, but he begins to speak as if he is going on a boat trip to make his fortune with Ben. He then speaks as if he were coaching Biff at American football again, and he has clearly lost all sense of time and proportion. He turns to face the audience momentarily as if they were the people in the stands watching the football.

The music rises to an unpleasant pitch to express Willy's confused mental state. Biff rushes downstairs as Willy leaves the house, and the noise of his car leaving at speed is heard. Music signifies that this is a moment of great emotion; it then quietens to the sound of one cello note repeated.

There is a sad tableau as all the remaining characters now prepare themselves in sombre fashion for Willy's funeral. The final gesture is left to Linda – she lays flowers at Willy's grave.

COMMENTARY

This final scene is where the whole family has to face the truth. Biff is prepared to admit defeat and leave the family home for ever. He has finally learnt how to live with the truth about himself and how to rid himself of expectations that he will never fulfil. He realises the impossibility of ever achieving Willy's personal dreams. Biff has grown to accept that he will not change his father.

The emotional climax is when Biff's love for Willy is made clear. This gives an opportunity to override Willy's dreams and to be reunited on a simple emotional level. Willy is delighted, but even this only strengthens his resolve to live out the American Dream on Biff's behalf. Biff's acceptance of his own responsibility should stop Willy from feeling obliged to do this, but it does not. Father and son love each other but cannot express their love properly. This is a tragic element. There is a feeling of inevitability about Willy's suicide: he has rationalised it with Ben, and he has also found a rational justification in the light of his love for Biff. Whatever anyone says now, it seems to Willy to be the only way out.

REQUIEM

- The family and friends express their feelings for the departed Willy.
- Linda is confused.
- Charley and Happy praise Willy, but Biff feels that his father wished for the wrong things.

CONTEXT
Willy's desire to pass on twenty thousand dollars to Biff is a sign that he dies still believing the capitalist doctrine that the main aim in life is the acquisition of wealth.

CONTEXT

A requiem is a special ceremony to honour the souls of the dead.

CHECK THE FILM

The final tableau in the Schlöndorff film, which shows the small group at the graveside, also reveals through subtle acting the differing attitudes towards Willy following his death.

Here the requiem is an opportunity to assess the validity of what Willy said about his funeral and to see the aftermath of his life. Willy predicted that his funeral would be well attended by all those who liked him, but this turns out to be a false hope. The belief that he was well respected is clearly unfounded. Linda has problems understanding Willy's motives for killing himself, and dwells on the good times. It seems particularly galling to her that they have just freed themselves of the financial burden of paying the mortgage. Happy intends to dedicate his life to his father by continuing to try to set up a company called the Loman Brothers. Biff gives him a look of despair at this point. He knows that Willy 'had the wrong dreams' (p. 110). Biff also states that his father did not understand himself. Charley alone is sympathetic to Willy and he eloquently expresses what it is like to live as a salesman: 'He's a man way out there in the blue, riding on a smile and a shoeshine' (p. 111). Charley argues that a salesman has to have a dream – it is in the nature of the job. Happy defends his father's dream 'to come out number-one man' (p. 111) and is determined to emulate his father. Linda is left to express her very sad feelings of bewilderment at Willy's death and her inability to cry, perhaps because she is both angry and sad.

COMMENTARY

'A salesman is got to dream' (p. 111), as Charley says. The reason why Willy cannot simply abandon his dreams and accept his son's love without aiming for greatness is that a dream is essential to his life. His sales techniques have finally infiltrated his consciousness to such an extent that he sells himself. Linda's statement, 'We're free' (p. 112), which is repeated three times, has many possible meanings. Willy is now free from earthly unhappiness. The couple are free from the need to earn money for the mortgage and, in another sense, the family is free to act without the pressure of Willy's dreams.

EXTENDED COMMENTARIES

TEXT 1 – TELLING WILLY THE NEWS (ACT II, PAGES 84–5)

WILLY: That so? What happened?

BIFF [*high, slightly alcoholic, above the earth*]: I'm going to tell you everything from first to last. It's been a strange day. [*Silence. He looks around, composes himself as best he can, but his breath keeps breaking the rhythm of his voice.*] I had to wait quite a while for him, and –

WILLY: Oliver?

BIFF: Yeah, Oliver. All day, as a matter of cold fact. And a lot of – instances – facts, Pop, facts about my life came back to me. Who was it, Pop? Who ever said I was a salesman with Oliver?

WILLY: Well, you were.

BIFF: No, Dad, I was a shipping clerk.

WILLY: But you were practically –

BIFF [*with determination*]: Dad, I don't know who said it first, but I was never a salesman for Bill Oliver.

WILLY: What're you talking about?

BIFF: Let's hold on to the facts tonight, Pop. We're not going to get anywhere bullin' around. I was a shipping clerk.

WILLY [*angrily*]: All right, now listen to me –

BIFF: Why don't you let me finish?

WILLY: I'm not interested in stories about the past or any crap of that kind because the woods are burning, boys, you understand? There's a big blaze going on all around. I was fired today.

BIFF [*shocked*]: How could you be?

WILLY: I was fired, and I'm looking for a little good news to tell your mother, because the woman has waited and the woman has suffered. The gist of it is that I haven't got a story left in my head, Biff. So don't give me a lecture about facts and aspects. I am not interested. Now what've you got to say to me?

> **CONTEXT**
>
> 'Projection' is a psychological term for attributing your own characteristics to someone else. Willy imagines his son was a salesman.

[STANLEY *enters with three drinks. They wait until he leaves.*]

WILLY: Did you see Oliver?

BIFF: Jesus, Dad!

WILLY: You mean you didn't go up there?

HAPPY: Sure he went up there.

BIFF: I did. I – saw him. How could they fire you?

WILLY [*on the edge of his chair*]: What kind of a welcome did he give you?

BIFF: He won't even let you work on commission?

WILLY: I'm out! [*Driving*] So tell me, he gave you a warm welcome?

HAPPY: Sure, Pop, sure!

BIFF [*driven*]: Well, it was kind of –

WILLY: I was wondering if he'd remember you. [*To* HAPPY] Imagine, man doesn't see him for ten, twelve years and gives him that kind of a welcome!

CHECK THE NET

http://www. thecrucibleonbroad way.com/bio_arthur _miller_aol_chat.asp features an online transcript of a conversation with Arthur Miller about *Death of a Salesman*.

How a central character like Willy Loman is played will depend on how his role is understood. Two contrasting ways in which he might be seen are the lyrical and the satirical. Lyric poetry expresses powerful personal feelings. A lyrical interpretation of Willy's role would bring out the sadness in his life and dignify it with meaning. It would be sympathetic to Linda's claim that 'attention must be finally paid to such a person' (p. 44).

The first English production starred Paul Muni as Willy. He was described by reviewers as 'a sad little chap, beaten from the start', and he played the role for all the pathos he could find.

The original American production on Broadway featured Lee J. Cobb in the role of Willy and he was a large man, describable as a 'walrus' to use the play's term (p. 29). Lee J. Cobb could not really represent a pathetic character, and instead he combined great presence and power with a crushing defeat. Lee J. Cobb's playing of Willy was impressive in his downfall and made the salesman seem a strong character. This style of acting became the dominant approach in America and it elevated Willy to more heroic proportions. In

England, Warren Mitchell, better known as the belligerent Alf
Garnett, has played the part.

Dustin Hoffman, a much smaller man than Lee J. Cobb, had the
text corrected to describe him as a 'shrimp' rather than a 'walrus'. In
Dustin Hoffman's performance, Willy was far less impressive and
his errors were much more apparent. Dustin Hoffman said he was
going to be a 'spitfire', spewing forth venom as the boys describe
their father in the play.

It is also possible to see the play as a biting condemnation of Willy's
attitudes. If we do not approve of Willy, it is possible to see him as a
moral coward who avoids all the real issues in order to inhabit a
dream-world where he can safely ignore other people's feelings. In
this case he should heed Biff's advice to 'take that phony dream and
burn it before something happens' (p. 106). On this interpretation,
Willy might be powerful and dangerous although always ready to
doubt and pity himself.

It is essential in studying the text to consider the possibility of
several different interpretations. What may appear to be a clear
meaning can be vastly different if the lines are pronounced
differently and from a different perspective. This passage offers an
example of how different interpretations of Willy's role might be
arrived at. The belligerent, powerful Willy Loman would be
concerned to impose himself on his boys yet again, and to cut short
any attempt at undermining him. There may even be an element of
conspiracy in the desire to find some good news to tell Linda. It
could sound as if he needed to feed her some comfort as the boys
do to him. So strong is the desire for reassurance that Willy
overrides Biff's anxieties. When Biff asks who it was that called him
a salesman, Willy's reply can either be a savage riposte, which
sounds as if he wants Biff to stop this nonsense, or it could be
spoken with great bewilderment as if he is mystified by the
question. The weak Willy who is cracking up would be eager for
good news for his own sake, and would most likely be surprised
and puzzled by this remark.

The sentence 'What're you talking about?' would be spoken
accusingly by the dynamic Willy, and defensively by the Willy who

CHECK THE BOOK

For an account of
the play's theatrical
history, see Bernard
F. Dukore, *Death of a
Salesman and The
Crucible: Text and
Performance* (1989),
and Brenda Murphy,
*Arthur Miller: Death
of a Salesman* (1995).

may be realising that he has been creating a falsehood all these years. The strong Willy is anxious to bend the boys to his way of thinking, whereas the weak character is so desperate that he has lost control of reason. Willy's angry 'now listen to me' may be a reaction in the strong character to a challenge to his authority; the alternative is to see this as Willy trying to put things in perspective, by offering what appears to be the most important news. In the speech where Willy says 'I was fired today', emphasis can be given to the pronoun 'I' or the word 'fired'. The dynamic Willy would be likely to emphasise the word 'I', suggesting that he wants to tell the boys that he has suffered something worse than Biff. The weak Willy might emphasise the word 'fired' to suggest that this explains his reason for not wanting to digress and go into Biff's past.

'Now what've you got to say to me?' can be issued as a challenge by a Cobb-type Willy, who wants his boys to support him as they have always done. In this case he is asking for obedience. For the weaker interpretation, the question is not a challenge, but a pathetic suggestion that he is finished and there is, indeed, little that can be said. The weak Willy would be pleading for understanding, whereas the Cobb-type Willy would be demanding compliance with his will.

CHECK THE BOOK

See Arthur Miller, *On Politics and the Art of Acting* (2001), for a discussion of the implications of acting styles.

It is important to remember that any play offers opportunities to actors to interpret their character differently and readers should not assume that the interpretation which seems obvious is the only possible one.

TEXT 2 – PLAYING YOUR HAND (ACT I, PAGES 34–9)

> [UNCLE BEN, *carrying a valise and an umbrella, enters the forestage from around the right corner of the house. He is a stolid man, in his sixties, with a moustache and an authoritative air. He is utterly certain of his destiny, and there is an aura of far places about him. He enters exactly as* WILLY *speaks.*]
>
> WILLY: I'm getting awfully tired, Ben.
>
> [BEN'S *music is heard.* BEN *looks around at everything.*]
>
> CHARLEY: Good, keep playing; you'll sleep better. Did you call me Ben?

[BEN *looks at his watch*.]

WILLY: That's funny. For a second there you reminded me of my brother Ben.

BEN: I only have a few minutes. [*He strolls, inspecting the place.* WILLY *and* CHARLEY *continue playing*.]

CHARLEY: You never heard from him again, heh? Since that time?

WILLY: Didn't Linda tell you? Couple of weeks ago we got a letter from his wife in Africa. He died.

CHARLEY: That so.

BEN [*chuckling*]: So this is Brooklyn, eh?

CHARLEY: Maybe you're in for some of his money.

WILLY: Naa, he had seven sons. There's just one opportunity I had with that man …

BEN: I must make a train, William. There are several properties I'm looking at in Alaska.

WILLY: Sure, sure! If I'd gone with him to Alaska that time, everything would've been totally different.

CHARLEY: Go on, you'd froze to death up there.

WILLY: What're you talking about?

BEN: Opportunity is tremendous in Alaska, William. Surprised you're not up there.

WILLY: Sure, tremendous.

CHARLEY: Heh?

WILLY: There was the only man I ever met who knew the answers.

CHARLEY: Who?

BEN: How are you all?

WILLY [*taking a pot, smiling*]: Fine, fine.

CHARLEY: Pretty sharp tonight.

BEN: Is Mother living with you?

WILLY: No, she died a long time ago.

CHARLEY: Who?

BEN: That's too bad. Fine specimen of a lady, Mother.

WILLY [*to* CHARLEY]: Heh?

BEN: I'd hoped to see the old girl.

CONTEXT

To take a pot means to take the pool of accumulated bets in a card game.

CHECK THE FILM

The way in which Willy's conversation is with both Charley and Ben at the same time is neatly portrayed in the 1985 film.

CHARLEY: Who died?

BEN: Heard anything from Father, have you?

WILLY [*unnerved*]: What do you mean, who died?

CHARLEY [*taking a pot*]: What're you talkin' about?

BEN [*looking at his watch*]: William, it's half past eight!

WILLY [*as though to dispel his confusion he angrily stops CHARLEY's hand*]: That's my build!

CHARLEY: I put the ace –

WILLY: If you don't know how to play the game I'm not gonna throw my money away on you!

CHARLEY [*rising*]: It was my ace, for God's sake!

WILLY: I'm through, I'm through!

BEN: When did Mother die?

WILLY: Long ago. Since the beginning you never knew how to play cards.

CHARLEY [*picks up the cards and goes to the door*]: All right! Next time I'll bring a deck with five aces.

WILLY: I don't play that kind of game!

CHARLEY [*turning to him*]: You ought to be ashamed of yourself!

WILLY: Yeah?

CHARLEY: Yeah! [*He goes out.*]

WILLY [*slamming the door after him*]: Ignoramus!

BEN [*as WILLY comes toward him through the wall-line of the kitchen*]: So you're William.

WILLY [*shaking BEN's hand*]: Ben! I've been waiting for you so long! What's the answer? How did you do it?

BEN: Oh, there's a story in that.

[LINDA *enters the forestage, as of old, carrying the wash basket.*]

LINDA: Is this Ben?

BEN [*gallantly*]: How do you do, my dear?

LINDA: Where've you been all these years? Willy's always wondered why you –

WILLY [*pulling BEN away from her impatiently*]: Where is Dad? Didn't you follow him? How did you get started?

BEN: Well, I don't know how much you remember.

WILLY: Well, I was just a baby, of course, only three or four years old –

BEN: Three years and eleven months.

WILLY: What a memory, Ben!

BEN: I have many enterprises, William, and I have never kept books.

WILLY: I remember I was sitting under the wagon in – was it Nebraska?

BEN: It was South Dakota, and I gave you a bunch of wild flowers.

WILLY: I remember you walking away down some open road.

BEN [*laughing*]: I was going to find Father in Alaska.

WILLY: Where is he?

BEN: At that age I had a very faulty view of geography, William. I discovered after a few days that I was heading due south, so instead of Alaska, I ended up in Africa.

LINDA: Africa!

WILLY: The Gold Coast!

BEN: Principally diamond mines.

LINDA: Diamond mines!

BEN: Yes, my dear. But I've only a few minutes –

WILLY: No! Boys! Boys! [YOUNG BIFF *and* HAPPY *appear.*] Listen to this. This is your Uncle Ben, a great man! Tell my boys, Ben!

BEN: Why boys, when I was seventeen I walked into the jungle, and when I was twenty-one I walked out. [*He laughs.*] And by God I was rich.

WILLY [*to the boys*]: You see what I been talking about? The greatest things can happen!

BEN [*glancing at his watch*]: I have an appointment in Ketchikan Tuesday week.

WILLY: No, Ben! Please tell about Dad. I want my boys to hear. I want them to know the kind of stock they spring from. All I remember is a man with a big beard, and I was in Mamma's lap, sitting around a fire, and some kind of high music.

BEN: His flute. He played the flute.

> **CHECK THE FILM**
> The 1985 film version starring Dustin Hoffman shows how Ben's laughter should be delivered.

WILLY: Sure, the flute, that's right!

[*New music is heard, a high, rollicking tune.*]

BEN: Father was a very great and a very wild-hearted man. We would start in Boston, and he'd toss the whole family into the wagon, and then he'd drive the team right across the country; through Ohio, and Indiana, Michigan, Illinois, and all the Western states. And we'd stop in the towns and sell the flutes that he'd made on the way. Great inventor, Father. With one gadget he made more in a week than a man like you could make in a lifetime.

WILLY: That's just the way I'm bringing them up, Ben – rugged, well liked, all-around.

BEN: Yeah? [*To* BIFF] Hit that, boy – hard as you can. [*He pounds his stomach.*]

BIFF: Oh, no, sir!

BEN [*taking boxing stance*]: Come on, get to me! [*He laughs.*]

WILLY: Go to it, Biff! Go ahead, show him!

BIFF: Okay! [*He cocks his fists and starts in.*]

LINDA [*to* WILLY]: Why must he fight, dear?

BEN [*sparring with* BIFF]: Good boy! Good boy!

WILLY: How's that, Ben, heh?

HAPPY: Give him the left, Biff!

LINDA: Why are you fighting?

BEN: Good boy! [*Suddenly comes in, trips* BIFF, *and stands over him, the point of his umbrella poised over* BIFF'S *eye.*]

LINDA: Look out, Biff!

BIFF: Gee!

BEN: [*patting* BIFF'S *knee*]: Never fight fair with a stranger, boy. You'll never get out of the jungle that way. [*Taking* LINDA'S *hand and bowing*] It was an honour and a pleasure to meet you, Linda.

LINDA [*withdrawing her hand coldly, frightened*]: Have a nice – trip.

BEN [*to* WILLY]: And good luck with your – what do you do?

WILLY: Selling.

CONTEXT

The connection between being liked and being successful was famously argued in Dale Carnegie's book, *How to Win Friends and Influence People* (1936).

BEN: Yes. Well … [*He raises his hand in farewell to all.*]

WILLY: No, Ben, I don't want you to think … [*He takes* BEN'S *arm to show him.*] It's Brooklyn, I know, but we hunt too.

BEN: Really, now.

WILLY: Oh, sure, there's snakes and rabbits and – that's why I moved out here. Why, Biff can fell any one of these trees in no time! Boys! Go right over to where they're building the apartment house and get some sand. We're gonna rebuild the entire front stoop right now! Watch this, Ben!

In this section of the play Ben appears to Willy as he is playing cards with Charley. Ben is fourteen years older than Willy and Willy is recollecting the fateful meeting when Ben asked him to go to Alaska. The actual refusal is enacted in Act II (p. 67). A meeting from the distant past is played out in the present, creating a 'montage' dialogue (see **Theatrical techniques** on **Montage**). Ben is in his sixties, which means that the encounter took place in the early 1930s. Willy has just remarked to Charley that 'A man who can't handle tools is not a man', but Ben enters with all the trappings of a white-collar worker. He carries a small case and an umbrella. His point of entry has to be just as Willy says that he is getting tired. Ben's entry occurs immediately after the remark to Charley and suggests that one of the memories that Willy represses is of a man who was unfamiliar with tools, yet was not 'disgusting'. Willy in fact envies Ben. Ben's behaviour, however, leaves a lot to be desired. He is supercilious and patronising. He clearly has little respect for his brother and emphasises his supposed superiority. It should be remembered that Ben is not intended to be a realistic character and has been played as a ghostly manifestation.

Willy's first speech to Ben is to tell him that he is awfully tired. This indicates that he shares confidences with his elder brother. It could even be a plea for pity. The conversation does not, however, take place entirely in Willy's head. His words are heard by Charley, who responds to them. The spectacle for the audience is meant to be moving. Here we have a man who has lost his ability to distinguish between past and present. His mind is disintegrating. Ben remains on stage as the game of cards between Willy and Charley continues.

QUESTION
Would you agree that the process of Willy's mind determined the pattern of the play?

It transpires that Ben has recently died. He is inspecting Willy's life. Since he is not a real character, we can interpret this as evidence of Willy's state of mind. He is concerned about status and what Ben would say to him if he saw his present condition. Ben's strolling inspection makes him appear contemptuous of Willy's relatively modest surroundings. The sentence 'So this is Brooklyn' implies that he might have expected more from Brooklyn. Chuckling only adds to the contempt. There is no objective reason to suppose Ben would have behaved in this way, hence we infer that Willy believes that status would have been uppermost in Ben's mind. Willy did refuse Ben's offer to go to Alaska and work for him, so it might be argued that Ben has a certain moral right to see how well Willy has done. Willy insisted that he was destined to do well with his company. The appearance of Ben is also a judgement on Willy.

As Willy tells Charley that he had one opportunity with Ben, we see what it was. Ben refers to the Alaskan venture. One of the glaring contradictions in Willy, however, is that although he feels that Ben knew all the answers at that point, he does not take the opportunity that he offers him. In terms of classical tragedy, this is the **hamartia**, the fatal flaw or error that precipitates the disaster. Everything would have been totally different if Willy had gone, but Ben is not an endearing character, and Willy might have sacrificed his good points to emulate him.

Willy takes his winning from the card table, the pot, as Ben asks how his family is. In symbolic terms, Willy is trying to impress Ben in order to justify his decision not to go to Alaska. Ben asks about their mother and Charley hears the reference to death, but Willy does not accept that any such reference has been made. At this point, we must begin to wonder whether Willy is deliberately deceiving Charley, or whether even he is unaware of what he is saying. Charley now takes the pot as if the fortunes are suddenly reversed. Willy then disputes whose cards are which and Charley is outraged. In the confusion, Willy makes the ambiguous statement 'I'm through, I'm through!' He may be finishing the game or expressing his despair, or both. Willy is able to maintain a reasonably coherent dialogue on the borderline between past and

---

CHECK THE BOOK

George Steiner's *Death of Tragedy* (1961, revised edition 1975) details aspects of the classical Greek theory of tragedy.

present but this delicate balance is easily upset. At the mention of his mother's death, Willy mingles past and present in an incoherent sentence: 'Long ago [referring to his mother's death]. Since the beginning you never knew how to play cards.' It is not clear whom Willy is referring to. It is possible that he is blaming himself for not 'playing his cards right' in life, but the effect is to alienate his only friend. The scene shows that living in the past destroys the present.

CONTEXT

The lament for the dead mother and the failure to connect with the late father are characteristic of Freud's Oedipal complex.

Willy now approaches Ben through the wall to signify that the sequence is imagined. This is now wishful thinking. We learn from Linda's remark that this is meant to be Ben's hoped-for return from Africa, which did not happen. Willy is now imagining making amends by discovering Ben's 'secret' – the source of his success. Willy is now almost sycophantic in his admiration of Ben. In response, Ben still arrogantly prides himself on his outstanding memory. When Willy and Linda express their astonishment at hearing that Ben made his fortune in diamond mines, he adds, 'But I've only a few minutes'. This signifies that he is aware that they are about to question him at length, and he dismisses the prospect. The memory of their dead father is neglected, in favour of the riches that Ben has made. The memory of the father is the emotional link which, like Biff's love for Willy, is more important than money. Willy, however, is unable to re-establish his connection with his father. He calls his boys to hear Ben's story to inspire them to achieve the same American Dream. Ben, however, simply states the bald facts: 'when I was seventeen I walked into the jungle, and when I was twenty-one I walked out. [*He laughs.*] And by God I was rich.' The refusal to explain how this happened, together with the sardonic laughter, again implies that he has no intention of passing on the secret.

Willy asks for more details of his father. He wants the boys to know what kind of 'stock' they come from. Ben's description of their father and his flute-making is actually very different from the American Dream as conceived by Willy. Ben even disparagingly adds that it was more financially rewarding. Willy, however, sees this story as a confirmation that he is bringing his sons up in the right way, 'rugged' and 'well liked'. His blinkered vision is clear to us here.

Ben's challenge to Biff to hit him is a response to this reference to masculinity. If the episode began with a reference to the lack of masculinity, Ben now proves that he is more virile than might be supposed. In knocking Biff down, however, he cruelly reminds Willy that his sons are not as rugged as he might think. Ben has an advantage here as well. In Willy's mind, Biff is unsuccessful because he cannot quite match the manly qualities that Ben is able to display with such ease at his age. Linda becomes cold towards Ben after he knocks down her son, but Willy has not recognised Ben's manner as patronising. The reference to selling gives Ben a line which can be used to show complete contempt for the occupation. It is with the mention of selling that Ben leaves. Since Ben is a figment of Willy's imagination at this point, this may signify a repressed shame about his profession.

> **CONTEXT**
>
> In psychoanalytic theory, a repressed emotion such as shame usually returns in another form, such as a hallucination.

TEXT 3 – ASKING THE BOSS A FAVOUR (ACT II, PAGES 59–64)

[HOWARD WAGNER, *thirty-six, wheels on a small typewriter table on which is a wire-recording machine and proceeds to plug it in. This is on the left forestage. Light slowly fades on* LINDA *as it rises on* HOWARD. HOWARD *is intent on threading the machine and only glances over his shoulder as* WILLY *appears.*]

WILLY: Pst! Pst!

HOWARD: Hello, Willy, come in.

WILLY: Like to have a little talk with you, Howard.

HOWARD: Sorry to keep you waiting. I'll be with you in a minute.

WILLY: What's that, Howard?

HOWARD: Didn't you ever see one of these? Wire recorder.

WILLY: Oh. Can we talk a minute?

HOWARD: Records things. Just got delivery yesterday. Been driving me crazy, the most terrific machine I ever saw in my life. I was up all night with it.

WILLY: What do you do with it?

HOWARD: I bought it for dictation, but you can do anything with it. Listen to this. I had it home last night. Listen to what I picked up. The first one is my daughter. Get this. [*He flicks the switch and 'Roll out the Barrel' is heard being whistled.*] Listen to that kid whistle.

WILLY: That is lifelike, isn't it?

HOWARD: Seven years old. Get that tone.

WILLY: Ts, ts. Like to ask a little favour if you …

[*The whistling breaks off, and the voice of* HOWARD'S *daughter is heard.*]

HIS DAUGHTER: 'Now you, Daddy.'

HOWARD: She's crazy for me! [*Again the same song is whistled.*] That's me! Ha! [*He winks.*]

WILLY: You're very good!

[*The whistling breaks off again. The machine runs silent for a moment.*]

HOWARD: Sh! Get this now, this is my son.

HIS SON: 'The capital of Alabama is Montgomery; the capital of Arizona is Phoenix; the capital of Arkansas is Little Rock; the capital of California is Sacramento …' [*and on, and on.*]

HOWARD [*holding up five fingers*]: Five years old, Willy!

WILLY: He'll make an announcer some day!

HIS SON [*continuing*]: 'The capital …'

HOWARD: Get that – alphabetical order! [*The machine breaks off suddenly.*] Wait a minute. The maid kicked the plug out.

WILLY: It certainly is a –

HOWARD: Sh, for God's sake!

HIS SON: 'It's nine o'clock, Bulova watch time. So I have to go to sleep.'

WILLY: That really is –

HOWARD: Wait a minute! The next is my wife.

[*They wait.*]

HOWARD'S VOICE: 'Go on, say something.' [*Pause.*] 'Well, you gonna talk?'

HIS WIFE: 'I can't think of anything.'

HOWARD'S VOICE: 'Well, talk – it's turning.'

HIS WIFE [*shyly, beaten*]: 'Hello.' [*Silence.*] 'Oh, Howard, I can't talk into this …'

HOWARD [*snapping the machine off*]: That was my wife.

CHECK THE FILM

The 1985 film directed by Volker Schlöndorff, starring Dustin Hoffman as Willy and John Malkovich as Biff, shows Willy addressing his remarks to Howard's chair, which is lit with a white light when he leaves the room, emphasising Willy's desperation.

WILLY: That is a wonderful machine. Can we –

HOWARD: I tell you, Willy, I'm gonna take my camera, and my bandsaw, and all my hobbies, and out they go. This is the most fascinating relaxation I ever found.

WILLY: I think I'll get one myself.

HOWARD: Sure, they're only a hundred and a half. You can't do without it. Supposing you wanna hear Jack Benny, see? But you can't be at home at that hour. So you tell the maid to turn the radio on when Jack Benny comes on, and this automatically goes on with the radio …

WILLY: And when you come home you …

HOWARD: You can come home twelve o'clock, one o'clock, any time you like, and you get yourself a Coke and sit yourself down, throw the switch, and there's Jack Benny's programme in the middle of the night!

WILLY: I'm definitely going to get one. Because lots of time I'm on the road, and I think to myself, what I must be missing on the radio!

HOWARD: Don't you have a radio in the car?

WILLY: Well, yeah, but who ever thinks of turning it on?

HOWARD: Say, aren't you supposed to be in Boston?

WILLY: That's what I want to talk to you about, Howard. You got a minute? [*He draws a chair in from the wing.*]

HOWARD: What happened? What're you doing here?

WILLY: Well …

HOWARD: You didn't crack up again, did you?

WILLY: Oh, no. No …

HOWARD: Geez, you had me worried there for a minute. What's the trouble?

WILLY: Well, tell you the truth, Howard. I've come to the decision that I'd rather not travel any more.

HOWARD: Not travel! Well, what'll you do?

WILLY: Remember, Christmas-time, when you had the party here? You said you'd try to think of some spot for me here in town.

HOWARD: With us?

CONTEXT

Howard's suggestion that Willy should buy a tape recorder shows that he is unaware of his staff's living standards; it is far too expensive for a man with Willy's income. This reflects the conspicuous consumption of luxury goods which capitalism encourages.

WILLY: Well, sure.

HOWARD: Oh, yeah, yeah. I remember. Well, I couldn't think of anything for you, Willy.

WILLY: I tell ya, Howard. The kids are all grown up, y'know. I don't need much any more. If I could take home – well, sixty-five dollars a week, I could swing it.

HOWARD: Yeah, but Willy, see I –

WILLY: I tell ya why, Howard. Speaking frankly and between the two of us, y'know – I'm just a little tired.

HOWARD: Oh, I could understand that, Willy. But you're a road man, Willy, and we do a road business. We've only got a half-dozen salesmen on the floor here.

WILLY: God knows, Howard, I never asked a favour of any man. But I was with the firm when your father used to carry you in here in his arms.

HOWARD: I know that, Willy, but –

WILLY: Your father came to me the day you were born and asked me what I thought of the name of Howard, may he rest in peace.

HOWARD: I appreciate that, Willy, but there just is no spot here for you. If I had a spot I'd slam you right in, but I just don't have a single solitary spot.

[*He looks for his lighter,* WILLY *has picked it up and gives it to him. Pause.*]

WILLY [*with increasing anger*]: Howard, all I need to set my table is fifty dollars a week.

HOWARD: But where am I going to put you, kid?

WILLY: Look, it isn't a question of whether I can sell merchandise, is it?

HOWARD: No, but it's a business, kid, and everybody's gotta pull his own weight.

WILLY [*desperately*]: Just let me tell you a story, Howard –

HOWARD: 'Cause you gotta admit, business is business.

WILLY [*angrily*]: Business is definitely business, but just listen for a minute. You don't understand this. When I was a boy – eighteen, nineteen – I was already on the road. And there was

CONTEXT

When Willy says he has never asked a favour of any man, he is clearly lying.

Text 3 – ASKING THE BOSS A FAVOUR (Act II, pages 59–64) continued

a question in my mind as to whether selling had a future for me. Because in those days I had a yearning to go to Alaska. See, there were three gold strikes in one month in Alaska, and I felt like going out. Just for the ride, you might say.

HOWARD [*barely interested*]: Don't say.

WILLY: Oh, yeah, my father lived many years in Alaska. He was an adventurous man. We've got quite a little streak of self-reliance in our family. I thought I'd go out with my older brother and try to locate him, and maybe settle in the North with the old man. And I was almost decided to go, when I met a salesman in the Parker House. His name was Dave Singleman. And he was eighty-four years old, and he'd drummed merchandise in thirty-one states. And old Dave, he'd go up to his room, y'understand, put on his green velvet slippers – I'll never forget – and pick up his phone and call the buyers, and without ever leaving his room, at the age of eighty-four, he made his living. And when I saw that, I realized that selling was the greatest career a man could want. 'Cause what could be more satisfying than to be able to go, at the age of eighty-four, into twenty or thirty different cities, and pick up a phone, and be remembered and loved and helped by so many different people? Do you know? when he died – and by the way he died the death of a salesman, in his green velvet slippers in the smoker of the New York, New Haven, and Hartford, going into Boston – when he died, hundreds of salesmen and buyers were at his funeral. Things were sad on a lotta trains for months after that. [*He stands up.* HOWARD *has not looked at him.*] In those days there was personality in it, Howard. There was respect, and comradeship, and gratitude in it. Today, it's all cut and dried, and there's no chance for bringing friendship to bear – or personality. You see what I mean? They don't know me any more.

HOWARD [*moving away, toward the right*]: That's just the thing, Willy.

Howard's entry with the '*wire-recording machine*' shows that he is unaware of the seriousness of Willy's situation. His fascination with

CONTEXT

It is clear that the funeral of this salesman, Dave Singleman, is the inspiration for Willy's later vision of his own send-off.

the technology may seem cruelly thoughtless at this point. It is ironic that as Willy attempts to ask Howard a favour, it is Howard's love for his family that intervenes and prevents him from acknowledging Willy's request. The daughter's voice asking for her father to speak suddenly drowns out Willy's voice. Howard's love for his daughter is, of course, just as strong as Willy's love for Biff, and here it becomes a barrier between Howard and Willy. This mirrors the situation elsewhere in the play when Willy allows his love for his son to create a barrier between himself and others. The fact that Willy allows the son's voice to continue at length without interruption signifies that he may have realised how intense Howard's love for his children is.

Willy's replies at this point may be either sarcastic or humble according to the way in which he is played. When he says of Howard's whistling, for example, 'You're very good!', this appears to be a rather insincere compliment. It may, of course, be Willy joking with Howard. When he says, 'That's me!' with a wink, this could be interpreted as a jovial attempt at humour, since the difference between his whistling and his daughter's is apparent. Howard's refusal to allow Willy to interrupt the recording of his wife stammering a few words is an indication of how his sentimentality can also be cruelty to others. Howard could be played at this point as rather foolish and thereby elevate Willy's status. When Willy says of the tape recorder, 'I think I'll get one myself', there is an opportunity for the performer to speak ironically. The recordings have been tedious, hence for Willy to say this might well be insincere. This would emphasise his command of the situation at this point. On the other hand, an actor who adopts the humble approach might well make such a line into an obsequious compliment.

Howard remarks that the machine is 'only a hundred and a half' if Willy wants to buy one. This inconsiderate remark ignores the fact that Willy would need to pay at least two weeks' income to buy one. It is clearly beyond his means but Howard does not acknowledge this. He even assumes that Willy will also have a maid, showing that he is oblivious to the financial pressures on his salesmen.

 CHECK THE NET

See http://www. public.iastate.edu/ ~spires/Concord/ deathsearch.html for a database containing the complete dialogue from the play, indexed and connected to its textual context to enable you to search for word lists and collocations.

Text 3 – ASKING THE BOSS A FAVOUR (Act II, pages 59–64) continued

Jack Benny was a radio comedian, and Willy appears to warm to the idea of recording programmes because he might miss them whilst driving. He is, of course, trying to steer the conversation towards the difficulties of his job and his need to change it. Howard's simple response is to suggest that Willy listens to the radio in the car. Again he misses the implication that Willy is on the road during the evening when he might be enjoying his leisure.

When Willy states that he never thinks of turning the radio on, this is a giveaway. Howard suddenly becomes aware of the superficial nature of Willy's responses, and he then asks why Willy is not in Boston. Willy asks if Howard has got a minute but simultaneously draws a chair closer. He can see that he has Howard's attention. Howard suspects that Willy may have not completed his job in Boston properly. The boss's neglect of Willy's feelings has now become clear. He does not seem to be worried about Willy's crack-up for Willy's sake alone. When Willy states that he does not want to travel, Howard's response implies that this means that Willy will give up work altogether. He is a salesman and nothing but.

Howard's confession that he was unable to come up with a position in town for Willy is a definite rejection, but Willy now is not listening. He continues as if it is a sales negotiation and drops the price. He is willing to work for less and less. In the middle of the negotiation, Howard searches for his lighter, and Willy gets it for him and gives it to him. This could either be a bold move on Willy's part, which draws attention to Howard's lack of awareness, or another obsequious gesture. He could even light the cigar to emphasise his subordinate position. It is at this point that Howard refers to him as 'kid' despite the fact that Willy is considerably older than him. Howard's position is a brutally pragmatic one: 'business is business'. In other words, the only consideration is whether the move for Willy will increase profits. Willy, however, seems to take up the reference to youth and begins a tale of when he was a boy. This might be a regression to a juvenile fantasy, or a criticism of the much younger boss attempting to impart worldly wisdom which he doesn't have. It can be played either way. The story is an attempt to establish a sense of brotherhood between the salesmen: Willy, Dave Singleman and Howard. The powerful speech evokes the sentimental tale of a man who made the profession respected and loved. Willy's love for his family, which is channelled into career endeavour, is confused with the occupation of selling. To a certain extent, this is a threat to Howard. Willy is reminding him of how he might feel if Willy dies and he feels responsible. When Willy stands, however, Howard '*has not looked at him*'. For Howard, the emotive story has no place in the negotiation. He must ignore the protest or be shamed or embarrassed by it. The act of standing can be an assertive gesture. It is almost symbolic of showing respect for the dead salesman of Willy's story, and a challenge to Howard. Can he be so heartless as to refuse to stand as well?

Willy's final comment on the moral of his own story – 'In those days there was personality in it' – is a self-defeating argument. Today personality does not count, and Willy only reminds Howard of this. What's more, he does not even have the personal relations he prides himself on. Either way, he is finished with Howard.

CONTEXT

When Willy refers to 'personality', he seems to mean the ability of a salesman to use charm to get what he wants.

PART THREE

CRITICAL APPROACHES

CHARACTERISATION

WILLY

Willy is meant to be played as someone who, to use the playwright's words, has '*massive dreams*', but also indulges in '*little cruelties*' (p. 8). Arthur Miller has defended Willy's character by arguing that he does have values. Despite his age and the hardship he has endured in the selling business, he dreams that he would be in charge of the New York sales area if the former boss were still alive. Willy would especially like to have his own business so that he could spend more time with his family. On the other hand, he berates his highly sympathetic wife for getting the wrong cheese. He seems unable to comprehend the fact that she was trying to please him. Both his dreaming and his cruelty suggest that Willy lives in a world of his own. He has unrealistic dreams of his own and his family's importance and he is unable to understand why other people do the things they do. In Biff's case, he is still puzzled as to why Biff is working on a farm, and this leads to a great deal of friction.

Willy's views are also liable to sudden change. In the space of a few lines, he says that Biff is 'a lazy bum' and then that he is 'not lazy' (p. 11). He is able to idealise Biff one moment and attack him viciously the next. One of the things that Willy treasures most in Biff is his former skill at polishing the car! This shows a failure to grasp Biff's true nature. At the age of thirty-four, Biff seems unlikely to discover talents which have lain hidden all this time.

Willy might also be considered a hypocrite. In his remarks to Biff about not getting too involved with women because they are gullible (p. 21), he is trying to lecture Biff on a moral fault of which he is guilty. As we later see, he has a mistress. Immediately after his advice to Biff about involvement with women, he then rejoices in the fact that the women pay for his son. This might be an indication that Biff deceives and exploits women, yet Willy is happy at the thought. When as a young sportsman, Biff 'borrows' a football from school, Willy tells him that he wants the ball to be returned,

CHECK THE BOOK

For Miller's views on Willy, see his introduction to his *Collected Plays* (1958), reprinted in *Plays: One* (Methuen, 1988).

yet he also argues that Biff's theft of the ball is somehow acceptable (p. 23). He both condones the theft and rejects it; this is not perhaps a sign of insincerity, but rather of his willingness to reinterpret events to fit his dreams.

One question about Willy is whether he is intent on pleasing himself or whether he is really concerned about the needs of others. At one point he says: 'when business is bad and there's nobody to talk to ... I get the feeling that I'll never sell anything again, that I won't make a living for you [Linda], or a business, a business for the boys. There's so much I want to make for' (p. 29). His love for Biff is heartfelt, but his ambitions for his son seem to have little relation to his son's needs and desires. His neglect springs directly from his dreams.

QUESTION
Biff says of Willy: 'He had the wrong dreams' (p. 110). Is this true?

A salesman lives by his ability to engage other people and make them believe in him, and this carries over into Willy's private life. He even tells lies to his wife about the sales he has made to appear to be earning a great deal of money. The news of the family's debts comes as a surprise to Willy, who refuses to face this reality.

Willy appears egotistical, claiming that he is supremely popular with his clients (p. 24) and telling his young sons that he can park his car in any street in New England and the police will protect it. These boasts turn out to be ill-founded. Willy's pride in his son Biff's ability to play sport and be admired is rooted in his belief that 'the man who makes an appearance in the business world, the man who creates personal interest, is the man who gets ahead' (p. 25).

Yet despite his apparent self-confidence, Willy tells his wife frankly about his fears and weaknesses. He has become aware of colleagues mocking him. Despite his belief in popularity and fighting talk, Willy can see that other men who say less are better salesmen: 'A man oughta come in with a few words. One thing about Charley. He's a man of few words, and they respect him' (p. 28). It may be that Willy needs to exaggerate to boost his self-confidence – a necessary part of a salesman's psychological equipment. Linda's reassurance shows how fragile Willy's self-respect is. He appears to depend on her support to survive, and when she says that he is 'idolized' by his sons (p. 29), we the audience know this not to be

CONTEXT
Willy's self-doubt, which breaks through his confidence on occasion and cannot be assuaged, is a classic symptom of depression.

true. Yet without this reassuring statement, Willy might not be able to face the next day.

Linda's support does not prevent Willy from having an affair with another woman. He tells Linda that he wants to 'kiss the life outa you' on the road (p. 29), but it is another woman that he kisses when he is lonely away from home. Willy's reason for the affair – that he is 'lonely' and has no one to talk to – is shown to be untrue, yet there is truth in the fact that he cannot communicate with his own family. Willy's attitude to Linda mending her stockings suggests he does harbour hidden feelings of guilt about his behaviour.

Willy's strongly held beliefs about his job affect his attitude to others. Although in some ways a proud man, he does accept charity. Yet while he is willing to accept money from Charley and even ask for an increase in the donation, he refuses the offer of a job and insults his friend. Willy is a competent builder and regards it as an essential manly virtue to be able to handle tools, yet he prefers to be a salesman. A salesman may achieve something big, whereas an ordinary worker, however secure the job, will never earn large amounts. Willy is disparaging about Happy's secure and reasonably well-paid job. Willy asks the figure of his dead brother Ben about his father because he knew him so little. Willy's father made and sold flutes – a minor trade, yet it led to creditable success and happiness.

Willy lacks self-awareness, a fact amply demonstrated when Biff decides to go to his former employer, Bill Oliver, to ask for a loan to start a business. At the end of Act I the entire family is in accord over the proposed business scheme, and the future is beginning to look rosy. Once again Willy stresses that it is the salesman's manner and behaviour that will win the day:

> Don't be so **modest**. You always started too low. Walk in with a big laugh. Don't look worried. Start off with a couple of your good stories to lighten things up. It's not what you say, it's how you say it – because personality always wins the day. (p. 51)

Willy projects his own behaviour and anxiety onto Biff. Willy himself will often look worried and start off too low in any negotiation. He is also a joker, and he knows that everyone loves a

CHECK THE BOOK

Raymond Williams, in *Drama from Ibsen to Brecht* (1968), says that 'it is not the image of Willy Loman as a man but the Salesman that predominates'.

joker but they don't lend him money. It should have become clear to Willy that appearance and image are not the sole criteria for success.

Willy asks Bernard and Ben how they achieved the success which he so desperately envies. Willy's own recipe for success is related to Ben in a scene from the past, and in the light of experience it seems woefully inadequate:

> it's not what you do, Ben. It's who you know and the smile on your face! It's contacts, Ben, contacts! The whole wealth of Alaska passes over the lunch table at the Commodore Hotel, and that's the wonder, the wonder of this country, that a man can end with diamonds here on the basis of being liked! (pp. 67–8)

Willy sways between vigorous assertion and intense doubt. When he is assertive, he frequently misses the point of all that we have seen acted on stage.

It is not easy to decide whether Willy refuses to face reality or is unable to do so. He does ask Bernard about Biff failing a maths exam and whether it was his fault (p. 73), which acknowledges the possibility, but he also seems to ignore the effect on Biff of finding him with his mistress. When Willy asks Biff about the meeting with Bill Oliver, his stubborn refusal to accept bad news is very clear. He will not recognise that Biff could have failed and he is unkind in his attitude, perhaps through desperation. The woman in the hotel describes Willy as 'self-centred'; as a person who dwells in his own dreams, he is liable to overlook the needs and aspirations of others. The rejection of Biff in the Boston hotel is unbearable and unfair. It is arguable that Willy is making others suffer for his inability to fulfil his dreams. The great sadness is that Willy believes he has to become supremely successful to earn Biff's love, when Biff has loved him all along. This is another example of how Willy's blindness can lead to disaster.

QUESTION
Is Willy a man whose problems stem from his inability to think about the problems of other people?

Part of Willy's appeal lies in the universality of some of his beliefs and concerns. For example, he attacks consumer society which has landed him in debt, raging against the shoddy goods that he is continually having to replace:

I'm always in a race with the junkyard! I just finished paying for
the car and it's on its last legs. The refrigerator consumes belts
like a goddam maniac. They time those things. They time them
so when you finally paid for them, they're used up. (p. 57)

These frustrations sound all too familiar and we identify with Willy
as an average citizen of the twentieth century.

Willy tends to ride the crest of emotional waves. When Linda tells
him that the boys would like to have a celebratory meal with him
after the business meeting with Bill Oliver, Willy's spirits are
renewed and he declares that he is going to be successful in his
meeting with his boss and come home with an advance sum of
money. When he does see Howard, however, Willy is unable to
interrupt Howard's trivial conversation about his new sound-
recording machine which Willy is drawn into praising. He does not
follow his own advice to Biff and allows himself to be put onto the
defensive. When Willy does get the chance to talk, he tells the story
of Dave Singleman in an attempt to appeal to Howard's emotions.
In this story, Willy reveals the source of the appeal of the selling
business for him:

> 'Cause what could be more satisfying than to be able to go, at the
> age of eighty-four, into twenty or thirty different cities, and pick
> up a phone, and be remembered and loved and helped by so
> many different people? Do you know? when he died …
> hundreds of salesmen and buyers were at his funeral. (p. 63)

Above all, Willy seems here to prize the emotional appeal of being
so popular, and it is social standing which really motivates him.
Willy becomes assertive, but he is clearly naive to suppose that this
argument will persuade Howard. His friendship with Howard's
father, demonstrated by the fact that he was asked for his approval
of the name Howard, does nothing to change Howard's mind.
Willy's nostalgia for the days when business involved 'respect, and
comradeship, and gratitude' (p. 63) is lost on Howard. Emotion has
no place in the world of commerce. When Howard fires him, Willy
resorts to calling on the boss's dead father, Frank. He returns in his
mind to the last strong emotional work relationship he had (with
Howard's father) as if that will save him from the sack.

CONTEXT

Willy's remark that
they should have
bought a 'well-
advertised'
refrigerator (p. 56)
suggests that he is
attracted to the
notion of material
goods as status
symbols, despite
his anger against
consumer society.

Willy can be seen as mistaken, malicious or simply misguided. Some of his errors derive from his own bizarre ideas, some from a desire to hurt or offend others, and some are misinterpretations of the messages which society sends out to him. He undoubtedly does have 'the wrong dreams' (p. 110) as Biff says, but he is also a man who works hard and wishes to do the best he can for his family. To condemn him outright would be as mistaken as believing that he has played no part at all in his downfall. Willy has courage of a kind and his one great quality is his persistence. He spends a great deal of time achieving very little and although his dreams may be misplaced, they have sustained him and enabled him to bring up a family. The play contains many sincere tributes to his courage and determination, the necessary virtues for success in any walk of life.

BIFF AND HAPPY

Arthur Miller has commented that he is sorry that 'Biff is not a weightier counterbalance to Willy's disaster in the audience's mind' (*New York Times*, 5 February 1950). This is to say that Biff's character should offer the basis for optimism to balance Willy's profound despair. Happy, on the other hand, seems more likely to reproduce the characteristics that his father displayed. He insists that he is going to show that Willy Loman did not die in vain and that he is going to 'win it' for him (p. 111). Yet competitiveness has already been shown in the play to be ultimately fruitless though it sustains the capitalist system. Biff's claim that his father 'never knew who he was' and that he himself does (p. 111) suggests that he will move away from his father's model for success.

An actor playing Biff has to take account of the transformation of this character throughout the play. Biff changes from a 'lost' boy, to a man of some insight and responsibility. Both brothers are described as '*lost*' when they are introduced (p. 14), but it is Happy who oozes confidence and refuses to give in throughout. Biff has lost confidence, according to Happy, and Willy is partly responsible for disparaging his farm work. Happy, on the other hand, has a good job and plenty of sexual power. Biff's problem is that he doesn't know 'what I'm supposed to want' (p. 16). Biff has spent six or seven years after high school trying to 'work myself up' and failing. He is eloquent on the lack of satisfaction to be found in a white-collar job:

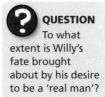

QUESTION
To what extent is Willy's fate brought about by his desire to be a 'real man'?

CONTEXT
Biff's dream of a life in the Golden West, the frontier of civilisation, echoes the increasing lack of freedom and opportunity in the industrialised cities.

BIFF AND HAPPY continued

To get on that subway on the hot mornings in summer. To devote your whole life to keeping stock, or making phone calls, or selling or buying. To suffer fifty weeks of the year for the sake of a two-week vacation, when all you really desire is to be outdoors, with your shirt off. And always to have to get ahead of the next fella. And still – that's how you build a future. (p. 16)

Biff sees himself as 'a boy' who is engaged in his hobbies rather than a career, and this causes him great anxiety every year as he gets older. Biff has lost his sexual confidence as he has grown older, whereas Happy has acquired more and more. It is arguable that all the Loman men need to grow up. Biff is able to express himself best when he paints a lyrical picture of farm life in Texas where he delivers colts.

Happy is aware that he has the kind of career that Biff despises. He can only wait for someone to die to achieve promotion. He is conscious that when his successful colleagues achieve their ambitions, they are not then fully satisfied and they continue to hunger. Happy also has all the things he could want at the present, but he too is dissatisfied. Everyone around him, according to Happy, is 'so false that I'm constantly lowering my ideals' (p. 18). When Happy describes his sexual morality, however, it is clear that he too is false. His relationships with women are a vengeful means of getting back at the men who have passed him on the career ladder. Referring to his ability to seduce women with ease, he remarks that 'it gets like bowling' (p. 18). He is, however, also ashamed of his behaviour and he would prefer to be honest. He will not take bribes, however easy the money might be, but he doesn't have any moral scruples about seducing a woman who is due to be married in five weeks (p. 19). Happy even expects to be called a bastard by his own brother when he tells him this. Happy's sexual competitiveness is the way in which he attempts to undermine the hierarchy of status within his company.

CONTEXT

Happy's comment that seducing women 'gets like bowling' recalls the phrase used at the time for passionate seduction: 'bowling someone over'. It implies that seducing women is easy for him.

Happy would like to create a Loman Brothers enterprise in farming where both brothers could lead the kind of lives they really enjoy. Happy would much rather compete with other men in direct physical terms such as boxing than in the psychological game of office politics. He entreats Biff to return and, like his father, whom he increasingly resembles, argues that Biff is 'well liked', as if this is enough to be successful. Scenes from the boys' early life show where they derived these attitudes.

Willy encouraged them to box, and we hear Biff ranking people according to whether they are 'well liked' (p. 25) in the way that Willy does (p. 23). The boys have both absorbed their father's ideas, but whereas Happy lives them, Biff is still trying to come to terms with the competitive ethos of capitalist society. Many of Arthur Miller's plays focus on the father-son relationship, and the impact Willy has on his sons is considerable. Biff competes on the sports field for Willy's sake.

? QUESTION
What signs are there that Happy and Biff will end up like their father?

Biff, however, is a thief, and he finds that his father condones these acts of stealing because in his eyes his son can do no wrong. He is quick to defend his sons when they steal wood for building the house, and this seems to lead Biff into a life of petty crime. Biff is able to criticise his father, however, and he becomes particularly critical when his mother is attacked. He accuses his father of never having had 'an ounce of respect' for Linda (p. 43), and he comments that Charley would never be seen 'spewing out that vomit from his mind' like his father (p. 44). Biff is angry that Willy is a 'fake', since he has known about his father's affair from the age of seventeen, but he does not reveal the details to Linda. He resolves to improve himself and gallantly kneels in front of his mother to make the promise. For Happy the prospect of success means that Biff will enjoy a good apartment and lots of women. As Biff makes his promise, so Happy also tells his mother rather foolishly that he is going to get married (p. 53).

In the restaurant as they wait for their father, Biff and Happy talk to a woman and Happy demonstrates a capacity to exaggerate like his father as he attempts to seduce her: 'Biff is one of the greatest football players in the country' (p. 81). Biff, however, has realised that the idea of getting financial backing from Bill Oliver was a delusion. He was hardly acknowledged and he now faces the reality that he had only been a shipping clerk and not a salesman as the family is fond of saying (p. 82). This revelation stuns Biff into the generalisation: 'We've been talking in a dream for fifteen years' (p. 82). Whereas Happy is busy constructing further myths, Biff is at last learning to overcome them. Biff clashes with Happy over their father and accuses his brother of not doing enough for him. Happy is willing to continue to hold out hope for his father by lying if necessary about the meeting with Bill Oliver, but Biff insists on frankness and tries to tell the full truth. Biff has had 'an experience' (p. 83), and he now knows that he was trying to achieve something that he knew to be worthless. In philosophical terms, Biff has discovered 'bad faith', the expression for the mental condition where we live according to others' expectations of us rather than our own needs and wishes. He states that 'all I want is out there, waiting for me the minute I say I know who I am!' (p. 105). Biff then asks his father why he cannot say who he is. Some kind of inhibition prevents him from hurting his father and destroying his illusions altogether until Willy rejects this kindness and insists on denying what Biff is saying. It is clear that Biff is sensitive and caring and loves his family deeply, but in the end the kindest thing he can do is to be cruel and force everyone to face the truth. This is why he reveals the fact that he has been in prison for theft.

Biff comes to an understanding of the mistakes he has made in wanting respectability and success on society's terms. Competitiveness and the desire for status are motives that do not fulfil the individual, and he blames himself for espousing these ideas which were imposed on him by his father. Biff goes on to try to make Willy face reality in his turn. It is Biff who says to Willy that there will be no pity for him if he chooses suicide (p. 104). At one point, he also states quite clearly that it was his father who 'blew me so full of hot air I could never stand taking orders from anybody!' (p. 104). It is the devastating statement that Biff and Willy are both 'a dime a dozen' (p. 105), or very ordinary, that shatters Willy's illusions. Now he has nothing to live for, because Biff finally knows who he is, and that he is not 'a leader of men' (p. 105). Once he frees himself of this psychological burden imposed by Willy, we might expect him to be capable of greater happiness, but Biff does not seem to understand how to live his life free from illusions, nor does he realise quite how they were insinuated into his own life by his father. We might expect Biff to free himself from guilt as well and blame his father for his own failures, rather than himself, but he does not do so. Perhaps this explains why Biff does not fully counterbalance the sense of doom that Willy's death causes. Biff has

CHECK THE BOOK

Eric Mottram writes about the Liberal notion of the free individual in his essay collected in *American Theatre*, edited by John Russell Brown and Bernard Harris (1967).

no programme for the future, but then, as he says, he is an ordinary man with no pretensions by the end of the play. Yet Biff appears to be the character who has the clearest understanding of what has gone wrong in the family and, in this sense, he perhaps represents some hope for the future.

LINDA

Linda is a staunch defender of everything that Willy stands for, yet she is also acutely aware of his nature: 'I know he's not easy to get along with – nobody knows that better then me – but ...' (p. 43). According to the stage directions, she is usually cheerful and has developed an '*iron repression*' of her objections to Willy's behaviour (p. 8). In other words, she is ready to excuse anything he does. Arthur Miller's opening stage direction suggests that she needs Willy to create ideals that she can believe in:

> *his massive dreams and little cruelties, served her only as sharp reminders of the turbulent longings within him, longings which she shares but lacks the temperament to utter and follow to their end.* (p. 8)

Willy may be irritable but he has set his sights on distant and worthwhile goals and gives Linda something to believe in. Linda mediates between Biff and Willy and tries to stop their arguments; in doing so, she often discovers the reasons for Willy's '*cruelties*'. In attacking Biff, for example, for not accomplishing anything, Willy is being cruel and inflicting misery on Biff, but his motive is to find his son a secure job where he will be respected:

> I'll see him in the morning; I'll have a nice talk with him. I'll get him a job selling. He could be big in no time. My God! Remember how they used to follow him around in high school? (p. 11)

Once Linda realises that this is the underlying motive for his petty cruelty, she turns to domestic matters and tries to calm Willy by offering him cheese that she has bought specially. This kindness is thrown back in her face without any justification, a rejection she accepts mildly.

? QUESTION
Despite his eventual death, is Willy an inspiration to many of the other characters because of his '*massive dreams*' (p. 8)?

The difficulty for an actress in playing Linda is to portray her as more than a spineless recipient of all Willy's foolishness and her sons' immaturity who has no worthwhile substance of her own. When she and Willy are discussing the loss of the trees which have been cut down in their neighbourhood, she ventures an opinion, but Willy abruptly denies her point without having the courtesy to consider it:

LINDA: Well, after all, people had to move somewhere.

WILLY: No, there's more people now.

LINDA: I don't think there's more people, I think –

WILLY: There's more people! That's what's ruining this country! (p. 12)

This conversation, however, has been prompted by the memory of the two elms where Willy once hung a swing and created a rural atmosphere. Linda comments that it was 'like being a million miles from the city' (p. 12). Willy's outburst is inexcusable in itself, but it again represents one of Willy's *'massive dreams'*, and it is this that makes him bearable.

In order to sustain Willy in his search to realise his dreams, Linda constantly supports his morale. She is, as Willy says, 'my foundation and my support' (p. 13). Linda knows that he tends to exaggerate his worries and 'make mountains out of molehills' (p. 13). In her own way, she, like Biff, is aware that Willy has impossible dreams, but she cannot allow herself to accept their impossibility. When Willy expresses grave self-doubt about his selling ability and his appearance, Linda's response recognises the need to bolster his self-confidence (p. 29). An actress playing Linda should distinguish between blind acceptance of Willy and all his faults, and gentle indulgence.

QUESTION
Is it true that the women in the play can see the men's faults more clearly than they can?

Linda has a clear and accurate vision of things in the play, yet cannot fully comprehend their implications. She alone is aware of the family's financial situation. She also tries to stop Biff from stealing, but is ignored: 'Don't let Biff ...' (p. 39). When it comes to crucial decisions, however, Linda shows an iron will. When she realises that the boys are not getting on with Willy, she is quick to offer an ultimatum:

He's the dearest man in the world to me, and I won't have
anyone making him feel unwanted and low and blue. You've got
to make up your mind now, darling, there's no leeway any more.
Either he's your father and you pay him that respect, or else
you're not to come here. (p. 43)

Linda's love sustains the family unit and she is determined that,
whatever he has done, Willy Loman must not be allowed to fall into
his grave 'like an old dog' (p. 44). When Biff reminds her that there
are many people who are worse off than Willy, Linda retorts that he
should make Charley his father. Her uncompromising attitude is
based on the absolute need to keep the family together. Linda
recognises what life on the road for a salesman is like, and she can
describe it in detail. She knows what drives Willy to extremes of
despair, and demands respect for his tenacity, if nothing else.

Linda is also aware that Willy intends to kill himself and has already
tried. She has the insight to understand that Willy's life is in Biff's
hands, as only he can restore Willy's self-respect. In many ways,
however, Linda is vulnerable to the actions of those about her and
does not have any means of changing her life independently. Linda's
one chance to deny the dreams that Willy entertains comes when
she rejects Ben's enticements to go to Alaska: 'Don't say those
things to him! Enough to be happy right here, right now' (p. 67).
Linda does not subscribe to all aspects of the American Dream, with
its masculine competitiveness and risk. This is not to say, however,
that she lacks strength. In contrast to her attitude towards the boys
at the beginning of the play, when she is delighted that they are
going out on a date (p. 10), she rounds on the sons when they return
from deserting Willy in the restaurant: 'Did you have to go to
women tonight? You and your lousy rotten whores!' (p. 98).
Linda's stature grows at this point and she is powerful in her final
defence of Willy. Her emotions hold until he is discovered
pathetically planting seeds in a barren backyard, and then sadness
overcomes her. She pleads, 'Will you please leave him alone?' (p. 99)
in an attempt to spare him the final humiliation of allowing his sons
to see him behaving like this. Linda could be played as a
downtrodden drudge, mending her stockings because she no longer
has any self-respect, but this would ignore the sharper and more
powerful sides to her character. She chooses to be passive when it

? QUESTION
Why is
there so little
attention paid to
Linda's tragic
statue?

seems appropriate and she is able to act decisively when it matters.
She is the strongest of all the characters.

BEN

Ben is to Willy's mind the epitome of all he desires: he calls him
'success incarnate' (p. 32). Ben went to Africa at the age of seventeen
and emerged rich from his work in diamond mines at twenty-one.
He is proof that, as Willy puts it: 'The greatest things can happen!'
(p. 37). As far as the audience is concerned, however, he is a
symbolic figure from Willy's mind, who represents all that Willy is
not. He is the opposite of Willy: self-assured, rich, adventurous and
not given to lengthy explanations. Willy regards his one great
mistake in life as not having accompanied Ben on a trip to Alaska
where he too might have made his fortune. When Ben does appear,
however, it is significant that Willy assures him of his own
happiness. The sentence 'I don't want you to think …' (p. 39)
indicates that Willy regards himself as being in competition with
Ben. The Loman family's rabbit-hunting is offered by Willy as an
example of his own wealth and success, but it seems tawdry by
comparison with Ben's time in the jungle.

**CHECK
THE NET**
For a list of
thought-provoking
study questions, see
http://mockingbird.
creighton.edu/
english/worldlit/
teaching/srp435/
miller.htm

Ben is asked for the secret of success by Willy but does not give any
kind of answer. His one moral lesson is to pretend to fight with Biff
and to trip him up unexpectedly, whilst holding his umbrella in
front of Biff's eye. The trick is meant to show that he will 'never get
out of the jungle' by fighting fair with a stranger (p. 38). The
reference to the jungle and its darkness calls to mind the phrase
'the law of the jungle', suggesting the necessity to be ruthless in a
ruthless world. The jungle that Ben speaks of, however, also
promises diamonds. Ben is an example of how to succeed in
capitalist society, by being competitive. As Ben puts it jokingly, the
stock exchange is also full of fearless characters (p. 39). In other
words the financial world is also like a jungle and it needs courage
to approach it.

When Ben next appears, Willy has just been rejected by Howard,
and Ben again uses fighting **metaphors** to explain how to succeed:

> I've bought timberland in Alaska and I need a man to look after
> things for me … You've a new continent at your doorstep,

William. Get out of these cities, they're full of talk and time payments and courts of law. Screw on your fists and you can fight for a fortune up there. (p. 66)

This speech echoes Biff and Happy's dreams of a farm in the country. This is the true pioneering spirit, which sees wealth as a reward for adventure.

Ben asks Willy to explain where the tangible rewards of his lifestyle are. The search for reputation and 'to be well liked' (p. 25) is not something that can be cashed in and Ben shows a hard commercial attitude towards Willy's philosophy. Ben tempts Willy with potential riches.

Ben fulfils his role as tempter in the scene where Willy is explaining that he wants to commit suicide in order to benefit Biff. Ben rejects the action, telling Willy that it is 'called a cowardly thing' (p. 100). By now, Ben's appearances are entirely imagined and show what Willy has retained from his previous conversations. On the other hand, to be consistent, Ben does agree that twenty thousand dollars is a very tangible argument, and in keeping with his businesslike approach he cannot deny that this has its attractions: 'that is something one can feel with the hand, it is there' (p. 100). Good personal relations and social standing are not something one can feel, of course. Ben's view of the suicide is 'A perfect proposition all around' (p. 107).

CHECK THE NET

See **http://www.homework-online.com/doas/index.asp** for more discussions on themes, characters analysis and important quotations, together with a user's forum where readers can ask and discuss questions about the play.

BERNARD

Bernard is Biff's cautious, studious, altruistic and law-abiding schoolfriend and is markedly different from him. Bernard partially fulfils the role of Biff's father by reminding him to study and not to drive the car without a licence. Whereas Biff is an accomplished athlete, Bernard is described by Willy as 'anaemic' (p. 25). Happy's response when Bernard comes to remind Biff that he should be studying for the public maths exam is to challenge him to a playful boxing match. This emphasises the fact that Bernard is not as strong or sporty as the Loman brothers. Bernard has accepted the realities of school life, but Willy dismisses him as 'not well liked' and lectures the boys on how Bernard will not succeed in the business world (p. 25). Bernard represents what Biff might have become without Willy's influence. When the adult Bernard appears he has matured into a successful lawyer with impressive credentials (he is about to plead a case before the Supreme Court) and wealthy friends.

Bernard's relationship with Biff was very close and he was particularly saddened by the fact that Biff did not retake his maths exam and qualify for university. He asks Willy about this, but Willy can now only defer to him and ask his advice. After the incident in Boston when Biff discovered his father having an affair, he burnt his sneakers which were already emblazoned with a university logo. Bernard had a prolonged fist fight with him at that point because of the apparent waste of talent which this represented: 'I've often thought of how strange it was that I knew he'd given up his life' (p. 74). Bernard is philosophical about success and advises Willy that giving up may sometimes be the best option. If you can't just walk away, he remarks, 'that's when it's tough' (p. 75). Bernard and Biff's relationship parallels Charley and Willy's. Bernard helps Biff academically, as his father helps Willy financially. Later in the play, when the young Bernard reappears to tell Mrs Loman that Willy has failed maths, he seems to represent Willy's nemesis: by this time we know that he is living evidence that Willy's advice to Biff was wrong.

CHECK THE BOOK
Some critics have suggested that the lengthy fight between Biff and Bernard has homoerotic overtones.

CHARLEY

If Bernard is the character who tries to make Biff face the reality of school life, then Charley is the one who tries to make Willy face the reality of working life. Charley seems to be Willy's only friend and he indulges him. Charley likes Willy, just as Bernard likes Biff, and he offers him a job, only to have it thrown back in his face by an angry Willy. He can see that Willy could change his life if he wanted to: 'I don't see no sense in it. You don't have to go on this way' (p. 34). Willy is remarkably rude to a man who gives him money, and Charley does not take as much offence as might be expected. Charley tries to persuade Willy to let Biff return to his farm job without worrying about him, and to accept the inevitable: 'When a deposit bottle is broken you don't get your nickel back' (p. 34). Willy, in his opinion, takes things too hard. Charley can see that Willy's skill at interior decorating is a worthy feature, and he respects Willy in many ways.

It is significant that Willy accidentally calls Charley Ben (p. 34). Charley is a living example of how to make a relative success of one's life, and Ben comes on stage in the middle of the conversation with Charley (p. 34). Charley tries hard to offer Willy good advice, but Willy can only express his frustration towards him, and even Charley concludes that Willy should be ashamed of himself. Charley lacks the practical skills that Willy associates with masculinity, and there is a suggestion that Charley admires him for qualities such as this. Charley is, or pretends to be, ignorant of football and can only joke about Biff's sporting success, much to Willy's annoyance. He has reason to admire the determined, masculine side of Willy.

In reality, however, the relationship between Willy and Charley is not very close. Charley accepts that they do not like each other. He can see one major flaw in Willy's character, which is that he is always boasting about what might have happened. When Bernard, Charley's son, leaves to go to the Supreme Court, Willy is amazed that he does not mention the fact that he is going to the most important court in the land. Charley replies that he doesn't have to because 'he's gonna do it' (p. 75). The implication here is that Willy constantly has to mention things which he will *not* eventually accomplish (such as starting his own business or making Biff into a sports star).

> **? QUESTION**
> Charley says to Willy that 'the funny thing is that you're a salesman, and you don't know that' (p. 77). Does Willy misunderstand the talents that a successful salesman should have?

Charley is down-to-earth and decent. Even Biff cites him as an example of someone who would not behave like his father (p. 44). When Willy begs money from him, Charley obliges, but when Willy increases his demands, Charley has to pause and think. He offers Willy a job, but finds it insulting that he will not accept it although he is begging money. When Willy becomes violent and threatens to fight him, Charley realises that he will not convince Willy. He is perhaps mistaken, however, to think that Willy is jealous of him (p. 77). Willy wants other things besides a secure existence, and Charley cannot comprehend this. He gives the example of a great financier, J. P. Morgan, and argues that he did not look impressive, but was greatly admired 'with his pockets on', when he could give people money (p. 77). All this is lost on Willy, however. Charley's salvation, according to him, 'is that I never took any interest in anything' (p. 75). Charley knows how dwelling on misfortune might only increase it.

HOWARD WAGNER

Howard's sole function is in the scene where he tells Willy that he no longer has a job (pp. 59–66). A successful man of thirty-six, he is not much older than Willy's sons. He wheels on a sound-recording machine and initially treats Willy very informally, demonstrating the machine and showing how much he loves his family when their voices are heard on the tape. Ironically, the more he revels in his humanity, the more he seems to crush the anxious Willy, who has come on what is, for him, vital personal business. Howard, is, in other words, not an inhuman person, and it has been remarked that Arthur Miller does not intend him to be criticised for firing Willy. This is a fact of life for the playwright: 'When a man gets old you fire him, you have to, he can't do the work' (quoted in Dennis Welland, *Miller: The Playwright*, p. 42). In such a businesslike context, emotion can play no part. Howard's explanation sounds reasonable, and we can believe that he has no alternative:

CHECK THE BOOK

In *Understanding Death of a Salesman: A Student Casebook* (1999) Brenda Murphy and Susan C. W. Abbotson provide contemporary historical documents which describe the attitudes of businessmen in this era.

> I appreciate that, Willy, but there just is no spot here for you. If I had a spot I'd slam you right in, but I just don't have a single solitary spot. (p. 62)

Howard offers an example of how Willy would be treated by someone without Charley's kindness. Howard decides what to do instantly and without allowing his emotions to affect his decision. He does not comment on Willy's stories of his dead father, but he does dispute Willy's sales figures. Howard represents what Willy can expect from the average member of business society and demonstrates that there is no sympathy for a man in this condition, although he does suggest that he will reconsider the position when Willy is feeling better.

THE WOMAN

The woman with whom Willy has an affair admires him, but she seems quite cold and unemotional. She sees being with Willy as 'good for me' (p. 30). She also says that she loves 'a lot of stockings' (p. 30). Willy gives her these as a present, but it is clear that she does not need them desperately. The picture begins to form that she is out to have a good time and benefit from her affair. She is one of the few people on whom Willy's charm actually works, but she emphasises that it was her decision to pick Willy because he made her laugh. The laughter that we hear from her throughout the play may begin to represent frivolity and meaninglessness. The affair is only a diversion for them both. She promises to put Willy 'right through to the buyers' (p. 30) when he next visits, so there is a suggestion of mutual interest in the relationship which makes it seem mercenary.

When the scene in the Boston hotel where the woman is discovered with Willy occurs, she begins to seem inconsiderate. The fact that she joins in the laughter when Biff is mimicking his maths teacher is highly uncomfortable and, given that she might be able to hear that it is Willy's son, very indiscreet. Her refusal to leave and her demand for more stockings make her seem selfish. Her laughter acquires the suggestion of someone who only wants to have a good time and considers morality irrelevant.

THE TWO GIRLS

Linda describes her sons' women as 'whores' (p. 98), but this is probably an exaggeration. The women, Letta and Miss Forsythe, are comparable to Willy's woman in the Boston hotel. Happy asks Miss Forsythe if she sells and she says, 'No, I don't sell' (p. 80), which could be taken as a question about prostitution. Miss Forsythe's responses to Happy's chat-up lines, with their ridiculous lies, may be similarly deceptive. Miss Forsythe says that she is a cover girl, a glamorous occupation which matches Happy's claim to be a champagne salesman. Biff, however, is obviously intimidated by her appearance, since he states that he 'could never make that' (p. 81). Happy seems to realise that the woman is insincere. He says that the reason why he cannot get married is because there are so many beautiful women to be attracted to and 'not a good woman in a thousand' (p. 81). This implies that he knows that she is not a good woman. Like Willy's woman, these two are also charmed by Happy's humour. The relationships created here show how shallowness is easy to exploit.

> **CONTEXT**
>
> The double standard prevalent at this time dictated that women should be sexually virtuous and men could excuse their infidelity; hence Willy's surprise to learn that the woman chose him.

> **CONTEXT**
>
> Happy's wish for a woman who displays 'resistance' (p. 19) is a reminder of Miller's theme that love is only possible when two people each retain their integrity.

THEATRICAL TECHNIQUES

REALISM

Despite the fact that Arthur Miller clearly departs from what we would recognise as **realist** techniques, he nonetheless believed that he was creating realist theatre. He has stated that realism consists in 'the nature of the questions asked and answered' (Introduction to *Collected Plays,* reprinted in *Plays: One,* 1988, p. 5), rather than style. The style of the play does not make it look exactly like real life. In real life people do not drift through walls, but this does not mean that the play does not reveal some crucial questions about humankind.

Arthur Miller felt that when a character was foremost on stage, then we had to accept this character as given. In classic Greek drama, characters such as Oedipus were taken for granted. In a realist play, according to Arthur Miller, we have the detail of the character's motives. This means that we can judge the central character's behaviour to be realistic because we see the reasons for the character's actions. Thus for Arthur Miller even Shakespeare can be judged to be realistic in his tragedies. What Arthur Miller valued most in Henrik Ibsen's style of nineteenth-century realism was what he called 'valid causation'. This is to say that if a play offers plausible and convincing reasons why characters are moved to act as they do, then it deserves the realist label.

CHECK THE BOOK

Raymond Williams gives a very incisive account of the play's realism in *Drama from Ibsen to Brecht* (1968).

This play is realistic in that the characters speak as American people of this era actually did, and do not have long, articulate speeches about their innermost motives. These two factors help to make us believe that we are watching something that corresponds with reality. At times, this can make the dialogue almost banal. In the Requiem, a poignant scene, Charley says of Willy, 'He was a happy man with a batch of cement' (p. 110). At such an emotional time, this might seem an inappropriate remark, yet ordinary people do not speak in poetic language.

The setting, the props and the costumes reflect the period in which the play is staged authentically. There are references to actual historical characters, such as Red Grange. Willy, for example, buys a punch bag for the boys with Gene Tunney's autograph on it. Tunney was a world-standard boxer, famous at the time.

In order to convince us that we are watching a complete and accurate portrayal of Willy's motives, it is important for the audience to be drawn into the spectacle. For this reason, the scene changes are subtle and attention is not drawn to them. The intention is to make the scene changes as imperceptible as the way in which the mind moves from one idea to another. The acting is also intended to be realistic and the dramatic illusion is not meant to be broken. The only moment in the play where there is a breach of the 'fourth wall' separating audience from player is when Willy looks towards the audience as if they were the people in the stands at Biff's football game. This can have the dramatic effect of accentuating his breakdown, but its impact is much greater because it is so unexpected. It does not destroy the overall illusion.

EXPRESSIONISM

A non-realist (but not *unrealistic*) element is that, as Arthur Miller says, '*Death of a Salesman* explodes the watch and the calendar' (Introduction to *Collected Plays*, reprinted in *Plays: One*, p. 6). In his attempt to expose the real motives of Willy Loman, Arthur Miller resorts to theatrical techniques that enable us to have a privileged glimpse into his mind. The original title of the play was to be *The Inside of His Head*. The playwright even contemplated a set on which a giant head opened up to reveal the action. In fact, the play gives us both internal and external views of Willy's motives. The collapsing of time so that Willy's memories and dreams become just as vivid as the immediate present is meant to indicate the state of a man's consciousness. Willy does entertain memories and sensations at the same time. This technique, however, gradually destroys the feeling that the play is primarily a narrative: a sequence of events governed by the laws of cause and effect. Arthur Miller believed instead that we should see all the inner complexity of the mind gradually revealed.

The theatrical technique that uses the stage to create a scene symbolic of the workings of a character's mind is **Expressionism**. *Death of a Salesman* fuses the realist and Expressionist styles with an ultimately realist purpose.

Expressionism as it was practised in Germany had many features that are echoed in this play. It moves forward as much through a progression of images as a clearly defined 'plot'. The work appeals

CHECK THE FILM
The 1985 film does not show transitions to the past in an Expressionist way, and this has been suggested as a reason for the film's failure in Miller's eyes.

primarily to the emotions, particularly a deep fear of modern life. It was a protest against society by an individual. In Walter Hasenclever's Expressionist play *The Son* (1914) a son reacts against the father who whips him and forms a league opposed to the ideology of the middle class. This is clearly echoed in Arthur Miller's play and shows the influence of Expressionism. The play's techniques are directed towards finding a means of negotiating a path from the inner world of the mind to the world outside. This could also be expressed as the perfect compromise between Expressionism and realism.

The Expressionist movement, however, was criticised for its portrayal of indulgent individualism. The theme of individualism is central to Arthur Miller's play. Willy appears to suffer dreadfully from the belief that the individual can change the world through his own mind. This fallacy costs Willy dear. Howard, for example, does not yield at all despite all Willy's salesman's tricks. Expressionists were attracted to the philosopher Friedrich Nietzsche's philosophy of nihilism, which denied all belief systems.

Nihilism was the belief that the world lacked any meaning. Friedrich Nietzsche's **metaphors** of nihilism – twilight, the bottomless abyss, madness and death – all fit Willy Loman. He finds his final chance of taking control of his life in ending it. This is a feature of what Nietzsche called 'the will to power'. In a world bereft of meaning the strong man creates it for himself. This is one aspect of Willy's character that we find admirable at times.

> **CONTEXT**
> Nietzsche wrote that he could measure the strength of a man's will by how much resistance, pain and torment it could endure.

Ultimately, however, Willy discovers that he cannot change the world by changing his mental attitude towards it. The will to power meets implacable opposition, and Arthur Miller does not espouse the Expressionist style wholesale.

STAGING

The staging of the play is crucial in establishing the effects which Arthur Miller wanted. The staging is a combination of the **naturalistic** – period furniture and props – alongside quite unnatural dream sequences. Arthur Miller's stage directions indicate that he wants the atmosphere created to be that of '*a dream rising out of reality*' (p. 7). The play is not explicitly divided into acts in order that the scene changes can be made as smooth as possible. When we suddenly see Willy speaking to a long-dead relative, it should come as a surprise and yet merge with the preceding conversation. This is to help to create the sense of witnessing the mental state of Willy, as if we were able to see into his mind. Lighting is therefore often used to make the transitions smooth. The lights will suddenly come up to focus on a different division of the house in order to designate a shift in time and space. The stage allows various spaces suddenly to 'become' another location. It also allows conversations to take place simultaneously. As time progresses, the staging also becomes symbolic. The oppressive apartment buildings which crowd around the house emphasise Willy's fear of the encroaching society and its 'competition'.

MONTAGE

Pure realism as a style, wrote Arthur Miller, seemed 'a defense against the assertion of meaning' (Introduction to *Collected Plays*, reprinted in *Plays: One*, p. 46). In other words, if the playwright restricted himself to showing everyday behaviour, then some of the relationships he wanted to expose could never be revealed. This is the reason why Arthur Miller mixes the changes in time with the entirely realistic sequences, in order to show relationships which we could not otherwise see. This technique owes a great deal to the technique of montage in the cinema, which was popularised by the Russian film-maker Sergei Eisenstein. Montage is the business of juxtaposing two images which would not normally be found side by side in real life to create a third meaning. This third meaning could not be expressed directly. An example of this occurs when Willy is protesting love for Linda and his family and says:

> WILLY: There's so much I want to make for –
>
> THE WOMAN: Me? You didn't make me, Willy. I picked you.
>
> WILLY [*pleased*]: You picked me? (p. 29)

The voice of the woman who is Willy's lover takes up the dialogue and creates a montage effect where we see Willy's earnest protestations of love and fidelity, alongside his delight at flattery from his lover. This creates the further effect of hypocrisy and shows how a man can entertain two conflicting ideas at once. On other occasions, the intervention of dialogue and sounds from the

CHECK THE FILM

The claustrophobic atmosphere of these encroaching buildings which hem in Willy's house is well illustrated in the 1985 film from the outset.

past creates a montage effect and enables us to see how Willy's mind is connecting ideas. When, for example, he discovers that Biff has walked off with Bill Oliver's pen, thereby ruining any chance of clinching a business deal with him, Willy hears sounds from the Boston hotel where Biff found him with another woman:

> BIFF: I never intended to do it, Dad!
>
> OPERATOR'S VOICE: Standish Arms, good evening!
>
> WILLY [*shouting*]: I'm not in my room! (p. 87)

Here the combination of Biff's theft and Willy's memory suggests that Willy sees this as retribution for his affair with the woman. Biff seems to be spiting him.

STRUCTURE

CHECK THE BOOK

Martin Esslin in *The Field of Drama: How the Signs of Drama Create Meaning on Stage and Screen* (1987) discusses the ways in which the structure of a play can be highly significant.

In his introduction to the *Collected Plays*, published in 1958 (and reprinted in *Plays: One*, 1988) Arthur Miller states that the structure of most of his plays is that a conflict is discovered and then clarified. One way of looking at it is that the play spends the first act in building up the idea of success which is so dear to Willy and the second act showing it being destroyed. Whereas the first act is full of dreams and expectations, the second one is full of truths and reckonings. The interpolated scenes from the past are sometimes called flashbacks as in film, but they gradually become confused with the present in Willy's mind, and confuse time zones. 'Daydreams' might be more appropriate a term. One effect of the switching of time is to allow us to see Willy's statements in an ironic light. Shortly after he has been dismissed by Howard, Willy returns in his thoughts to a discussion with Ben when he decided quite firmly not to go to Alaska. Then he says, 'I am building something with this firm' (p. 67). The cruel irony, of course, is that we have just seen all that he built destroyed.

THEMES

CAPITALISM AND THE VALUE OF LIFE

Death of a Salesman is the story of a man who comes to the conclusion that he can only save his life by losing it: Willy Loman eventually has to commit suicide to redeem himself in his own eyes and achieve something for his family. In this sense, the play is concerned with what Aristotle called a 'serious' action, involving life and death. The early responses to the play tried to assimilate it into the tradition of tragedy. The play suggests that tragedy may befall the most ordinary life in contemporary society, and for this reason it raises issues about the way we all live and work and dream of happiness. As Arthur Miller has written, the play represents the need to 'face the fact of death in order to strengthen ourselves for life' (Introduction to *Collected Plays*, reprinted in *Plays: One*, p. 33).

Despite the setting in 1949, many of the features of American society which it depicts are still with us. Arthur Miller's attack on the consumer society's constant attempts to sell us goods which do not serve our needs is still as meaningful now as it was in 1949, if not more so. The economic system of capitalism, where we are encouraged to accumulate capital as a symbol of success and a protection against disaster for our families, is familiar to today's audiences. From Europe to China, theatregoers have seen aspects of their own life enacted and voiced by Willy Loman. If this can be said to be a truly great play, its appeal may lie in the incisive vision of the mentality that capitalism can create in us. Willy finds that in purely financial terms he is worth more dead than alive. This, of course, is not an uncommon situation for some of us today. The insurance money he believes his family will collect if he dies may enable them to survive in much better conditions and realise the dreams he could not fulfil. On the face of it, therefore, to come to such a conclusion is a terrible indictment of the world in which we live. Arthur Miller writes in the introduction to his *Collected Plays* that Willy has broken the 'law of success' (reprinted in *Plays: One*, p. 35). Arthur Miller describes this as the law that a man who has failed in business has no right to live. In the essay *The Myth of Sisyphus* (1942), the French writer Albert Camus began by posing the fundamental philosophical question: why do we not kill ourselves? What, in other words, is the force or motivation that convinces us that life is better than death? Arthur Miller has said in his autobiography that he welcomed thinkers such as Jean-Paul Sartre and Albert Camus whose political stance owed nothing to Moscow, yet who showed how to avoid fascism in the post-war era. 'America was where you got rich but Europe was where the thinking was going on, or so you tended to imagine. America was becoming suspiciously unreal' (*Timebends*, p. 155).

**CHECK
THE BOOK**

In *Understanding Death of a Salesman, A Student Casebook* (1999) Brenda Murphy and Susan C. W. Abbotson discuss the contemporary culture which influenced salesmen such as Willy, and provide contemporary documents.

CAPITALISM AND THE VALUE OF LIFE continued

Willy Loman presents the ultimate challenge to an 'unreal' society which is based on capitalism, since he concludes that twenty thousand dollars is worth more than his life. Can a man really be valued at the amount of money which he is worth? If so, then capitalist societies such as America have reduced human beings to commodities, and dehumanisation is inevitable.

The play may expose weaknesses and contradictions in Willy's reasoning, but it is essential that we detect them. To accept Willy's logic that sacrifice is the price of his self-respect would be to accept a terrible truth. Audiences and readers feel the need to identify where Willy goes wrong and decide how this defeatist logic can be refuted. If the play is an indictment of our way of life, then it has profound implications for all societies which now embrace the ethos of capitalism. Arthur Miller's early flirtation with Marxism is often suspected to be an influence here, but he has explicitly rejected the idea that the play is overtly political. Whilst he obviously had sympathies with aspects of Communist thinking, he maintains that his work is much more than the sum total of its political implications.

AN ORDINARY MAN

CHECK THE NET

http://www.
bellmore-merrick.
k12.ny.us/
death.html is a
useful website that
discusses such key
issues such as
illusion versus reality
and dreams which
lead to denial.

For some critics, the play shows a central character who makes a number of rather obvious errors. Rather than being fascinated by his similarity with the majority of us, they see him as a particularly foolish man. Yet Miller has a cautionary note about this: 'the path is opened for those who wish to call Willy merely a foolish man even as they themselves are living in obedience to the same law that killed him' (Introduction to *Collected Plays*, reprinted in *Plays: One*, p. 36). If Willy were merely a foolish character, he would be unlikely to have earned the respect that has been paid to him. On the other hand, he is not clear-sighted and does labour under delusions. He might be said to represent humanity, with all its virtues and vices.

The play's appeal, however, seems to lie in its ability to characterise the ordinary man (the 'low man') and to ennoble him. It is almost because he is ordinary and recognisably subject to the same temptations as the rest of us that he becomes dignified. Willy may be making ordinary mistakes, but he is also fighting back against his fate in an unusual way. Willy Loman is sometimes full of contradictions, overly ambitious, blind to his vanities and unsympathetic towards those who love him. At other times, however, he is courageous, determined to the point of fanaticism, and almost a martyr to his family. It is this combination of seemingly incompatible qualities that makes Willy Loman a realistic and fascinating character. Arthur Miller himself laughed at the contradictions he built into Willy's character. Willy the salesman is the person who is most outraged about the way in which shoddy goods are designed to fall apart just as you have finished paying for them. As a salesman he has one set of values, and as a consumer he has another. Willy simultaneously provokes outrage at his behaviour while moving audiences to tears. The contradictions in Willy's character perhaps seem less strange now than they did in 1949, as inconsistency of character has almost become a hallmark of literature today. The view that we are pulled in different directions by social forces which work against each other has become increasingly accepted. Willy is not someone with a consistent core to his personality. We should not mock this, as Arthur Miller warns us that it may be a general human characteristic in today's society. The playwright uses Willy's words to describe himself in his autobiography:

> 'I still feel – kind of temporary about myself,' Willy Loman says to his brother Ben. I smiled as I wrote the line in the spring of 1948, when it had not yet occurred to me that it summed up my own condition then and throughout my life. The here and now was always melting before the head of a dream coming toward me or its tail going away. (*Timebends*, p. 69)

Nowadays it is generally recognised that the self is provisional: rather than being a fixed and stable entity which we can examine scientifically, it is always in the process of becoming something new. Willy acknowledges that he is discovering things about himself. The fact that Arthur Miller can acknowledge this same trait is an indication that it is perhaps neither unusual nor particularly foolish.

Arthur Miller's own position is that he is neither blaming society alone, nor presenting a pathetic character who is the author of his own misfortunes. The play, according to Arthur Miller, offers something between these two extremes – it is a study of how man and society interrelate. In China, the line where Willy defiantly announces, 'I am Willy Loman, and you are Biff Loman!' (p. 105)

www. CHECK THE NET
On http://www. thecrucibleonbroad way.com/bio_arthur _miller_aol_chat.asp Arthur Miller says that Willy's 'situation – his job, his boss, his life – is probably more typical than advertised'.

was seen as a counter to generations of a Communism in which individuals had no right to express themselves. However, this should not be seen as a triumphant assertion of victory either. In Willy, Arthur Miller has created a character who compels his audience to ask fundamental questions about human freedom and necessity which we can all recognise as significant. As Miller put it, 'the assumption was that everyone knew Willy Loman'.

LANGUAGE AND STYLE

The early **Expressionist** August Strindberg discovered that his *Dream Play* (1902), which contains scenes reminiscent of Arthur Miller's, could function well with the minimum of scenery and props. The spoken word alone could communicate the majority of information. This principle is followed to an extent in the staging of *Death of a Salesman*, since only the bare minimum of props needed to signify a kitchen is used, for example. There are many occasions in the play where a character has to convey the feel or mood of his or her emotions through language alone. Biff, for example, has to give some indication of the appeal of a rural life for him. The problem for the playwright is that he will be unable to make a character like Biff speak particularly eloquently. The language used is ordinary and it doesn't quite achieve the status of poetry, according to most critics, but it does have a memorable quality. Much of Willy's appeal derives from his concise expression of the inconveniences of modern life:

> The street is lined with cars. There's not a breath of fresh air in the neighbourhood. The grass don't grow any more, you can't raise a carrot in the backyard. They should've had a law against apartment houses. (p. 12)

The language may not be poetic, but it rings with strong emotion and is just as memorable at heightened moments.

SIGNS AND SYMBOLS

Arthur Miller has stated in his introduction to his *Collected Plays* (reprinted in *Plays: One*, p. 52) that he has 'stood squarely in

CHECK THE BOOK

See Stephen A. Marino's work *A Language Study of Arthur Miller's Plays* (2002) for a full discussion of linguistic features of the play.

conventional realism' but added to it, and one aspect of **realism** is that elements of the play become highly symbolic. In this play, for example, the stockings which Linda mends, but Willy gives to his lover, acquire a symbolic significance. They imply more than mere garments, and they begin to acquire the double meaning of self-indulgence or household drudgery. Biff is particularly moved by the fact that Willy gives his mother's stockings to his lover. Stockings were, at the time, highly prized and difficult to obtain, hence they represent a genuine concern for a woman. To give them to someone else implies a lack of regard for Linda. Some symbols on stage become vivid and extreme ways of illustrating the state of Willy's mind, in keeping with the Expressionism which influenced him. The best example of this may be the tape recorder which Willy accidentally sets in motion. In its shrieking, unpleasant tones of a child recounting meaningless phrases, we may see how awful it is for Willy to have to live with an accurate account of the past such as this. This is a vivid expression of his unconscious desire to repress the accurate facts.

Where language or even montage cannot convey meaning accurately or economically, Arthur Miller uses signs. A sign is anything which conveys meaning to the audience. Music is one obvious example, which acquires increasing meaning as the play continues. The sound of the flute at the beginning is of far less significance than at the end when it has picked up all manner of associations.

Music is used more like a film score to underline the obvious emotions. The flute is reminiscent of Willy's father and his relatively carefree existence, and the distant sound at one point, for example, prompts Willy to begin to reminisce about Biff's childhood and the red Chevvy car which he used to have. Other signs are created through gestures. At one point, as Willy begins to move from contemplating the present to evoking the past, his vision gradually becomes fixed on a point off-stage to indicate this. Linda unbuttoning Willy's coat as he buttons it suggests that he is becoming helpless and in need of support. In studying the play it is vital to remember that all these elements contribute to the meaning in addition to the spoken words.

? QUESTION
The first stage directions indicate that the play should appear like '*a dream rising out of reality*' (p. 7). Is this an accurate description of the whole play?

PART FOUR

CRITICAL HISTORY

TRAGEDY?

The most frequently discussed critical issue regarding this play is whether it can be called a tragedy. Biff calls his father a 'prince' (p. 90), and this evokes a possible comparison with Hamlet, prince of Denmark. Aristotle, the ancient philosopher, wrote the first, and in many ways the most significant, treatise on tragedy in his *Poetics*. Here he wrote that tragedy represents men as better than they are. The purpose of tragedy was to create pity and fear in the audience. This was achieved by showing us a fate that we feared and a character who deserved our pity for undergoing it. It could be argued that *Death of a Salesman* conforms to this pattern. Act I might be said to inspire horror as Willy's sad state is made clear, and Act II could engender pity as he suffers even more for it. Aristotle thought, however, that only people of high birth could be tragic heroes, since for a lowly born person to come to grief would not be so moving. The tragic hero was one who made one fatal mistake and then was severely punished out of all proportion to the mistake that was made. The **hamartia** or tragic flaw in the hero's personality caused him to suffer. His nobility was savagely destroyed by fate. To be a tragic hero in the Aristotelian sense, Willy would have to be a man of obvious virtue who has a tragic flaw that leads to a terrible fate. This would place the blame for the events of the play firmly on Willy's shoulders, even though the punishment is extreme.

We would normally also feel that the tragedy was a terrible waste of a valuable life. With nineteenth-century dramatists such as Henrik Ibsen, who wrote what is generally accepted as a tragedy in *Ghosts* (1881), the term was applied to the middle classes. *Ghosts* is a play about transmission of a sexually inherited disease from one generation to the next. Rather than defining tragedy as a fall from a great height, Ibsen helped to extend the concept to the ordinary person who becomes involved in a fate that they do not deserve and are not responsible for.

CHECK THE BOOK

See Harold Bloom's consideration of the comparison with King Lear in *Willy Loman* (1990).

Arthur Miller adapted Ibsen's play *An Enemy of the People* in 1950, shortly after writing *Death of a Salesman*, and was clearly influenced by the Norwegian. Miller has stated: 'I believe that the common man is as apt a subject for tragedy as kings are' (*New York Times*, 27 February 1949). In order for Willy to be a tragic victim in this sense, however, he must also be somehow admirable and potentially worthwhile, so that his demise can be seen as a waste and therefore tragic. Arthur Miller wrote that the corner grocer could be just as tragic as the president of the United States if he 'engages the issues of, for instance, the survival of the race, the relationships of man to God – the questions, in short, whose answers define humanity and the right way to live' (Introduction to *Collected Plays*, reprinted in *Plays: One*, p. 32).

The early responses to the play hailed it as a moving tragedy and a great success for that. The *New York Herald Tribune* described it as a 'soaring tragedy', with moments where Willy displays a 'touching grandeur' (quoted in *File on Miller* by C. W. E. Bigsby, p. 22). The *New York World Telegram* saw the play as a drama where Willy's fate is 'a destruction whose roots are entirely in his own soul' (ibid. p. 25). Despite the fact that Willy Loman's mistakes were clearly recognised, as Neil Carson writes:

> Lee Cobb particularly, a huge rumpled man with a deep, rich voice, endowed the character of Willy with a dignity beyond his station in life. It was Cobb's ability to lift his performance on to the high plane of tragic acting, to create a character that was exhausted without being weak, misguided rather than insane, that contributed so largely to the impact of the New York production. (*Arthur Miller*, p. 46)

There was undoubtedly something appealing in the elevation of an ordinary American to heroic status. It would enable many of the New York audience to feel that their own lives had to some extent been in some way dignified.

As Bernard F. Dukore also notes, the corresponding productions in London and Paris were not so emotional: 'London first-nighters failed to snuffle' (*Death of a Salesman and The Crucible: Text and Performance*, p. 65). Paul Muni's playing of Willy in London

CHECK THE BOOK
Death of a Salesman: Text and Criticism, edited by Gerald Weales (1996), is one of the many books and essays that discuss Willy's tragic status.

projected him as a man who was cracking up, a study in weakness and disintegration. The essence of the tragic interpretation is that Willy is seen as a man who is in control of his fate. He may be punished by forces beyond his control, but the error was committed by the character himself. To make such a character distinguished, the error must spring from a noble intention which is somehow thwarted. Then we can admire the character at the same time as blaming him. Lee J. Cobb's performance was undoubtedly a major factor in establishing a tragic stature for Willy.

HEROIC STATUS

George Steiner has written in *Death of Tragedy* (1961) that a contemporary audience can no longer accept that a tragic hero is punished by cosmic force unleashed by a mistake. We no longer believe in such underlying metaphysical forces, hence a tragedy must be brought about by the central characters themselves and by recognisable social factors. Tragic heroes nowadays, therefore, have autonomy: they are fully responsible for their actions, if not the consequences of those actions. The difficulty here is that the more responsibility is credited to Willy, the more foolish he seems. An Aristotelian tragic hero is overcome by external forces, but Willy clearly has the option of rejecting them. He can ignore advertising if he wants to. In Aristotelian tragedy, the drama ends with **catharsis**, the purging of our emotions as, for example, when the villain we have come to hate is finally punished. This feeling consolidates the view of classical tragedy that disaster can be averted if individuals are sufficiently cautious.

> **? QUESTION**
> Linda says of Willy: 'a terrible thing is happening to him' (p. 44). Is it true that Willy is enduring misfortune rather than ruining his life?

As critics began to consider the play at length, Willy was increasingly criticised. One English reviewer described Willy Loman as 'the little salesman with a pathetic belief in his worthless son' (J. C. Trewin in *Drama*, Winter, 1949). Arthur Miller himself had stressed the play's tragic intention and had argued for a broader definition of tragedy which would encompass Willy Loman. The essay 'Tragedy and the Common Man' was published in 1949 as the play was being produced (see *The Theater Essays of Arthur Miller*). Here Arthur Miller's approach is to argue that the common man may also gain 'size' by his willingness to 'throw everything he has into the contest – the battle to secure his rightful place in the world'. Total commitment, however, does not imply that a character is automatically endorsed by the audience. As Dennis Welland writes: 'Tragedy implies values' (*Miller: The Playwright*, p. 43). Critics have accused Willy of having no great values. After all, he does not really believe in any explicit faith or achieve any great works except, perhaps, paying off the mortgage. Arthur Miller, however, has responded by arguing that Willy does have *ideals*:

> Had Willy been unaware of his separation from values that endure he would have died contentedly while polishing his car ... But he was agonized by his awareness of being in a false position, so constantly haunted by the hollowness of all he had placed his faith in ... (Introduction to *Collected Plays*, reprinted in *Plays: One*, p. 34)

Values are clear systems of belief, whereas ideals may be vague notions of what could be achievable. It is arguable, however, that Willy does not die because he realises he cannot succeed in a great and worthwhile plan, but because death is the way he *will* succeed on his terms. Nobody makes Willy commit suicide. He is not under any illusions about his loved ones dying or a disaster caused by him. He seems to be free to act as he chooses and he acts wrongly,

It would be tragic if someone with good intentions died because he mistook the means of realising them, but not, perhaps, if a man with the wrong ideas fell foul of them. If Willy had the 'wrong dreams' (p. 110), as Biff says, then the tragic fate might seem to be deserved. The more we recognise Willy's freedom of action, the less admirable and tragic he seems. Arthur Miller eventually tired of arguing the case for Willy and regretted entering the debate. In answer to the accusations, the playwright has a subtle response. Willy may not have a clear vision of what he does wrong, but he is aware of an emptiness and a need in his life which his actions do not fulfil. Miller argues that to give the tragic hero a clear vision would be to give him the power to avoid his fate:

> it seems to me that there is of necessity a severe limitation of self-awareness in any character, even the most knowing, which serves to define him as a character, and more, that this very limit serves to complete the tragedy ... (Introduction to *Collected Plays*, reprinted in *Plays: One*, p. 35)

CHECK THE BOOK

Eric Mottram in his essay collected in *American Theatre* (1967), edited by John Russell Brown and Bernard Harris describes the heroic aspect of Willy as the 'thrust for freedom' exemplified here.

When Linda declares in the strangely rhythmic sentence: 'Attention, attention must be finally paid to such a person' (p. 44), she is making a plea to recognise the tragic quality of the play. This is almost Arthur Miller addressing the audience himself. Is Willy capable of wanting anything sufficiently important to make him truly tragic, or are his desires always petty? In the end, shouldn't we extend our concept of tragedy to include the unknown people who fail in life despite their enormous efforts?

Arthur Miller has written that 'to me the tragedy of Willy Loman is that he gave his life, or sold it, in order to justify the waste of it' (*New York Times*, 5 February 1950). Willy worked for others all his life, in other words, yet all this added up to was the opportunity to throw it away. Arthur Miller implies that the true tragedy is that Willy worked for nothing: ultimately his life lacked meaning, despite a frantic desire to find it. Miller has also said that it is tragic if a man's life is the price of his personal dignity. We recall Willy's desperate efforts to ask Ben, Charley and Bernard what the secret was. The difficulty is that we may find it hard to pity a person who is warned that they are wrong, persists, and eventually pays for their own errors. Even Charley, however, who can see this better than anybody, still declares: 'Nobody dast blame this man' (p. 111).

CONTEXT

Aaron Copland, the American composer, had written and performed the popular orchestral work *Fanfare for the Common Man* in 1942.

Willy, we must remember, is not intended to be a great man, and Arthur Miller denies that he set out to write a conventional tragedy. If we look for the usual characteristics of the genre of tragedy, we will not find them in this play. Miller has argued that there should be a number of formal definitions of tragedy, rather than one all-embracing **paradigm**. It could be argued that what makes Willy seem great at times is his refusal to rest content with what he is. Miller writes about 'the intensity of the human passion to surpass his given bounds'. Willy does have a fanatical desire to transcend his ordinariness. This may be an emotion with which audiences can sympathise. It also may take courage to persist in such an ambition, which also makes Willy seem more noble.

SOCIAL DRAMA

If Willy is not a tragic figure, then one alternative is that this is a play which sets out to show how society is structured to bring the good people to ruin, a social drama. The concept of a social drama and the concept of tragedy are almost mutually exclusive: if society is to blame, then Willy is not tragic because he does not bring disaster on himself. If society is not to blame, however, then it might appear, as it did to many critics, that Willy is simply foolish. As Eric Mottram said in 1967: 'His fate is not tragic … Everyone fails in a waste of misplaced energy' (*Arthur Miller: A Collection of Critical Essays*, edited by Robert W. Corrigan, p. 32).

At the other extreme, it has been argued that this is a play which sets out to expose the corrupting influence of American society. This would mean that Willy is not to blame, but that he is the victim. The play might still be considered tragic, but only in a much narrower sense. Then it would be tragic in the sense that any defeat of ordinary people by an inhuman system is. Contemporary Marxist sympathisers saw Arthur Miller as being confused by tragedy. For those who saw social conditions as the source of all blame, to accuse Willy of bringing disaster on himself was muddled. In the *Daily Worker*, in 1949, Lee Newton wrote: 'Ambiguity is not the result of clear thematic thinking' (quoted in *Death of a Salesman and The Crucible. Text and Performance* by Bernard F. Dukore, p. 19). Eleanor Clark, in *Partisan Review*, maintained that 'It is, of course, the brutal capitalist system that has done Willy.' Clark also argues, however, that 'it is our particular form of money economy that has bred the absurdly false ideals of both father and sons' (quoted in *Miller: The Playwright* by Dennis Welland, p. 39). The argument for this approach depends on the interview with Howard. This is undoubtedly a turning point in Willy's life, but Arthur Miller endorses Howard's attitude and it is not a permanent exclusion from work. Miller has avoided a propaganda play which simply sets out to accuse the American political system of being the cause of all ills. Marxist interpretations of the play, which accuse society of governing our behaviour, have been offered, but they have rested on the apparent inhumanity of Howard's treatment of Willy after so many years of service. As we have seen in the character study of Howard, this is not easy to sustain. Howard's dismissal of Willy can be seen as a response to his mental condition. After all, Howard does refer to his previous breakdown: 'You didn't crack up again, did you?' (p. 61).

www. CHECK THE NET
See **http://www. english.upenn.edu/ ~afilreis/50s/home. html** for a further look at the literature and culture of the American 1950s.

MAN IN SOCIETY

Although it might be wrong to see the play as a criticism of society alone, it does condemn many aspects of the social system. Although the **Expressionist** technique makes it focus on the psychology of the individual rather than social conditions, the conditions are evident. It would be extreme, however, to argue that Arthur Miller portrays a man who, in Marx's words, finds that 'social being determines consciousness'. Willy's dramatic presence makes it difficult to dismiss his own actions and to see him as a pure product of society rather than an instigator. The difficulty with the view that society is to blame is, as Neil Carson argues, that it 'simplifies the play' (*Arthur Miller*, p. 47). The playwright himself argues against any reduction of his play to political ideology, and reminds us that Charley, a capitalist, is the most 'decent' person in the play.

Arthur Miller believes that he cannot disentangle man from society and society from man. It is not a question of whether Willy *or* society is to blame, in other words. Miller wrote:

> I think that man is a social animal; there's no getting away from it. He's in society the way a fish is in water and the water is in the fish ... I'm under no illusion that people invent themselves. They do to a degree, but they're working in a social matrix ...

It may be that we do have free will, but that some of the social structures within which we operate are limited and constrain us. Arthur Miller here is alluding to Marx's statement that 'Men make their own fate but not in circumstances of their own choosing'. The Marxist drama critic, Raymond Williams, whose political criticism also stresses the interplay of the personal and the social, writing in 1969, praises Arthur Miller's 'drama of social questions' rather than *answers*. Raymond Williams argues that social **realism**:

> lies in a particular conception of the relationship of the individual to society, in which neither is the individual seen as a unit, nor the society as an aggregate, but both are seen as belonging to a continuous and in real terms inseparable process ... (*Arthur Miller: A Collection of Critical Essays*, edited by Robert W. Corrigan, p. 70)

QUESTION
Is *Death of a Salesman* such a celebrated play because of the questions it raises without any definitive answers?

Raymond Williams emphasises two important aspects of the play in Marxist terms: alienation and false consciousness. Willy has sold things for so long that he has begun to sell himself. This commodification of his own being distances himself from society and even his own family. He cannot reconcile the Willy who sells himself with the Willy who loves his family. The scene where he browbeats Biff in the restaurant to come up with some good news for his mother is an example. Here he wants to sell himself to Linda, just as he does when he overstates the money he has made. This, however, destroys his relationship with Biff. Alienation divides the self into dissonant elements. In trying to live up to ideals which have been found externally, Willy is living in the Marxist false consciousness, unaware of his alienation and willing to excuse it. Even Raymond Williams, however, acknowledges that the subtle balance between personal responsibility and social forces is not achievable without reconsidering the dramatic form, since we see things only from Willy's perspective (see the essay by Brian Parker, 'Point of View in *Death of a Salesman*', in *Arthur Miller: A Collection of Critical Essays*, edited by Robert W. Corrigan).

? **QUESTION**
Happy says that 'everybody around me is so false that I'm constantly lowering my ideals' (p.18). Is this remark true of Willy?

POLITICS

Criticism of the play has not extended much beyond these issues. The most fruitful directions suggested by the foregoing debates are still to be fully explored. The Marxist approach to the play, for example, would nowadays focus on the concept of ideology. The Marxist thinker Gramsci has argued that hegemony is the condition whereby a state maintains control of its people by subtly maintaining a dominance over the ideas which are popular. Hence Willy's belief in competition, which turns a law of his society into a law of nature, is an example of hegemony at work. It would be argued that it is in the interests of capitalist society to allow everyone to believe that they could succeed if only they tried. This would ultimately result in more productivity.

Ideology is argued to be a set of beliefs which are unconscious. This would coincide with Arthur Miller's theory that the tragic hero is only half aware of the forces which work on him. Criticism, therefore, has begun to explore some of the implicit contradictions which are not immediately apparent in Willy's character.

PSYCHOANALYSIS

It would be possible, for example, to see the play in Freudian terms, with the characters representing various aspects of Freud's mental model. Happy may represent unrestrained desire (the id), Linda the voice of society (the superego), and Biff and Willy both struggle to reconcile the two by developing an ego. Willy's repression of the past is a barrier to maturity and ego-development. (See the psychiatric work referred to in Dennis Welland's *Miller: The Playwright*, p. 48). Most of Willy's dream sequences are in fact manifestations of his unacknowledged desires. This underlying ferment would also account for the earlier descriptions of Willy as a person who is striving to discover his own identity (see Eric Mottram in *Arthur Miller: A Collection of Critical Essays*, edited by Robert W. Corrigan). Structuralist analyses have found that underlying the action, 'moral failures correlate with career failures' (*Practising Theory and Reading Literature: An Introduction* by R. Selden, p. 59; see also the essay 'Fantasy and Reality: Dramatic Rhythm in *Death of a Salesman*' by Leah Hadomi). This would suggest that the play's unconscious has its own structure for the American Dream.

CHECK THE BOOK

The American Dream is discussed by Gerald M. Burkowitz in *American Drama of the Twentieth Century* (1992).

THE FAMILY

It has been observed that the play is not entirely opposed to the American Dream, and in this respect it might be seen as reshaping the conditions necessary for success. If there is a contemporary ideology which Willy has absorbed, it is the belief in the family. The family is essential to the American way of life, and Engels argued that it was also the foundation of capitalism. Because families made people responsible for dependants, it also made them need more money. This enslaved them to capitalism where they could be exploited for profit. Marxist theories suggest that hegemony can be maintained by encouraging this kind of belief. Willy still wants to be responsible for Biff at an age where most fathers would have given up. He also believes that work such as selling and the family values of love and respect can be united. Dave Singleman is his model for this. He believes, in other words, that selling can fulfil the whole man. He does not recognise his alienation. In this way, ideology is damaging his nature.

GENDER

In his belief in the family, Willy also does not recognise that his vision is an essentially male one (See Kay Stanton's essay in *Willy Loman*, edited by Harold Bloom). Aristotle thought that valour in a woman was inappropriate for tragedy. Dennis Welland, however, argues that Linda is unrealistically good for such a play (*Miller: The Playwright*). In *Death of a Salesman* the women have no role to play which is not dependent on men. Linda's function seems to be to comment on and support Willy. The woman with whom Willy has an affair is not characterised except in so far as she relates to him, and Happy and Biff's two female associates are thinly sketched in order further to exemplify the sons' characters. When Willy considers suicide, he spares no thought at all for his wife, and it is left to the playwright to provide a poignant scene at the end where she shows the depth of her grief. It may appear that the women in the play seek men to define their existence and provide them with pleasure and direction. Linda, despite her courage and determination, offers little in the way of personal views on the events. Happy refers to seducing women as being like bowling. It is easy to strike at immobile, senseless targets, and many of the women referred to seem passive, waiting only for men to come into their existence and claim them. Only the woman in the hotel suggests that she has enough free will to choose Willy for an affair. This, however, may be to exonerate Willy, and to avoid casting him as a seducer like Happy. Women in the play seem to be either saintly like Linda, or whores like Willy's woman and the two women in the restaurant. These two stereotypes fulfil the male characters' needs at home and in bed, but they appear to have few, if any, needs of their own. Willy undermines the traditional family by treating women in this way. Happy too actively undermines the tradition of marriage. This is another example of the divergent forces operating in Willy's life.

Willy invites study from the post-structuralist point of view, as a character riven with such dissonant impulses that he is completely 'decentred'. Alongside his heterosexual behaviour, there are also signs of unusually close male relationships and homoeroticism which threaten to disrupt any conventional picture of the nuclear family. Willy and Charley have a very close relationship, in which Willy is given money by Charley and disparages him for his lack of

CHECK THE BOOK

For an account of how Willy both lives and thinks as a salesman, see Ronald Hayman, *Arthur Miller* (1970).

CONTEXT

It can be argued that both sons and Willy suffer bitterly from guilt as a result of failing to control their sexual urges.

CHECK THE BOOK

Anthony Easthope in *What a Man's Gotta Do* (1986) argues that in our culture the myth of masculinity demands that men should be masculine all the time and deny their feminine aspects (p. 19).

masculinity and threatens to fight him. (See *Feminist Theories for Dramatic Criticism* by Gayle Austin, and *Communists, Cowboys and Queers: The Politics of Masculinity in the Work of Arthur Miller and Tennessee Williams* by David Savran.) Gender is also a concept which is subject to divergent forces and becomes increasingly questioned in the play. In general, we might do well to remember Arthur Miller's remark that this play is about a man who has 'lost control of the forces of life', and this may be either because he is personally unable to retain his hold, or because it is slipping away from us all.

PART FIVE

BACKGROUND

ARTHUR MILLER

The playwright was born in 1915, and grew up during the American
Depression, the economic crisis of the 1930s when many enterprises
were bankrupted. Arthur Miller also records that many men called
at the door during this period asking to wash the windows and
some fainted from hunger. This left a deep impression on him
and a sense of responsibility and guilt. 'The Depression', wrote
Arthur Miller, 'is my book' (*Harper's* CCXVII, August 1958).
The economic climate affected his own family when his father's
clothing business experienced financial difficulties. Arthur Miller's
father employed nearly a thousand workers to make women's
coats. Arthur Miller himself worked briefly as a salesman, and his
experience as a schoolboy of working in a car parts warehouse for a
miserly sum is one which is clearly echoed in his plays. He was also
keen to learn about building, and he, like Willy, bought wood and
built a porch, as he recalls in his autobiography. Many of Arthur
Miller's plays focus on aspects of the Jewish experience, although
Arthur Miller's own Jewish background does not seem to feature
greatly in this play. The economic crash of the Depression put great
strain on relationships in the Miller family.

CHECK THE NET
http://web.archive.
org/web/
20010925134726/
http://deathofasales
man.com/ provides
information on
Robert Falls's
1999 Broadway
production of the
play, starring Brian
Dennehy as Willy.

On graduating from university having studied journalism, Arthur
Miller began to write plays and win awards. Eventually he
transferred to creative writing classes. *All My Sons* was produced in
1947 and ran for 328 performances. *Death of a Salesman* was
performed in 1949, ran for much longer and won the Pulitzer Prize.
With this success, Arthur Miller was established as a playwright. In
1953 he wrote *The Crucible*, a story of the persecution of witches in
the early America of 1692. The plot is a thinly disguised treatment
of contemporary events. Senator Joseph McCarthy was the leading
force in a campaign during the 1950s to bring to light any
Communists who existed in America. The unfairness of the
interrogations is cleverly revealed. In 1957 Arthur Miller was
brought before the Congressional Committee which investigated
'un-American activities' or Communism, and he refused to name
anyone who had expressed left-wing sympathies. He was convicted

CHECK THE BOOK

In his introduction to the Penguin edition of the play *The Crucible*, Miller wrote that in seventeenth-century New England 'the repressions of order were heavier than seemed warranted by the dangers against which the order was organized'.

of contempt of Congress. He admitted to having flirted with Communist ideas, but he did not believe that these ideas threatened the integrity of creative artists. The press respected him for his cool and dignified manner under interrogation. The conviction for contempt was reversed the following year by the Supreme Court.

It was at this point that Arthur Miller married Marilyn Monroe, whom he was to divorce five years later. In 1962 Arthur Miller married his present wife Ingeborg Morath, a photographer. Arthur Miller's career has continued and his stature as one of America's greatest playwrights has been consolidated, but *Death of a Salesman* is still for many his most memorable work.

HIS OTHER WORKS

Arthur Miller is a prolific writer, best known for his plays, which include *All My Sons* (1947), *The Crucible* (1953), *A Memory of Two Mondays* (1955), *A View from the Bridge* (1955), *After the Fall* (1964), *Incident at Vichy* (1964), *The Price* (1968), *The Archbishop's Ceiling* (1977), *The American Clock* (1980), *Playing for Time* (1981), which won the Peabody Award, *Two-Way Mirror* (1982), *Danger: Memory!* (1987), *The Ride Down Mount Morgan* (1991), *The Last Yankee* (1993) and *Broken Glass* (1994).

Other works include a novel, *Focus* (1945), a film screenplay, *The Misfits* (1961), a collection of short stories, *I Don't Need You Any More* (1967), and his autobiography, *Timebends* (1987).

HISTORICAL BACKGROUND

When it was first performed on Broadway, *Death of a Salesman* ran for 742 performances, and was a striking success. It made Arthur Miller's reputation and some thought it set the standard for American drama in general. Some critics were even moved to call this the American *King Lear*. Arthur Miller recalls that people were stunned after the first performance and then moved to lengthy, rapturous applause. Some people openly wept. One elderly man whom Arthur Miller saw being led from the theatre turned out to be a wealthy shop-owner, who gave orders that none of his staff were ever to be fired for being old. The corresponding performances in London and Paris were less ecstatic: much of the American style of the play would not be so familiar to international audiences in 1949, who did not know as much about America from the media as we do today.

CAPITALISM

On the opening night, Arthur Miller recalls that a woman angrily described the play as a 'time bomb under American capitalism' (quoted in *Timebends*, p. 184). Communist sympathisers, on the other hand, denounced it as failing to condemn American society. Arthur Miller rejects the view that this is a play explicitly designed to overthrow the social system of America. It aims rather to destroy the 'bullshit' of capitalism, 'this pseudo life that thought to touch the clouds by standing on top of a refrigerator' (*Timebends*, p. 184). In this expression, Arthur Miller describes the kind of social climate that was prevalent at the time. Capitalism as a political system depends on the continual encouragement of wants. People must want more and buy more in order to fuel the economy and enable people to work to produce these goods. Arthur Miller is disparaging about the capitalist system which encourages people to want more and more goods, such as refrigerators, as if this is the ultimate point of existence. Willy attacks consumer society with vigour in a way that is still relevant to our lives: he argues that machines are timed to collapse just as you finish paying for them. Linda, when questioned about the repairs to the washing machine by Willy, says, 'They [the washing machine company] got the biggest ads of any of them!' (p. 27). The fact that Willy can complain that the street is lined with cars indicates that he lives in a reasonably affluent neighbourhood. Willy can pride himself on the fact that the Chevrolet is 'the greatest car ever built' (p. 26) and treat it as a status symbol when it is working, and attack it when it needs repair: 'That goddam Chevrolet, they ought to prohibit the manufacture of that car!' (p. 28). The play describes the economic boom and increasing desire for material goods that followed the war. For anyone who had lived through the Great Depression of the 1930s, when it became clear that American society could not provide opportunities for all, and some might starve, this consumerism must have seemed a troubling development. The consequence is a spiritual vacuum and, to his credit, Willy notices this.

QUESTION
Discuss the view that the reason why an ordinary man like Willy Loman can be considered tragic is that all ordinary men lead tragic lives in a capitalist society.

THE AMERICAN DREAM

Willy is sensitive enough to notice how the neighbourhood has been changed for the worse by encroaching industrial society. He yearns for a more rural existence and condemns the claustrophobic atmosphere created by the increased building. Willy misses the elm trees and the flowers. On stage the set helps to establish this claustrophobic atmosphere. The social attitudes that Willy displays are those which were common at the time of writing. The American Dream offers the chance of riches even to those who start with nothing; it harks back to the early history of America, in which pioneers conquered the wilderness of the frontier. Ben represents this to Willy: 'There was a man started with the clothes on his back and ended up with diamond mines' (p. 32). The characteristics for success are thought to be masculinity, competitiveness and popularity. The myth was that becoming rich was a simple matter of using your personal qualities as an individual. The other great myth that prompted people to work hard was that America was the land of *opportunity*. The logic of these myths is that failure to achieve the American Dream must indicate a failure of personality. Arthur Miller notes in his autobiography:

> It has often been said that what kept the United States from revolution in the depths of the Great Depression was the readiness of Americans to blame themselves rather than the system for their downfall. (*Timebends*, p. 113)

There are clear echoes of this attitude in Willy and Biff, who both blame themselves for their lack of economic success and its repercussions for the family.

Something of the pioneer spirit of the early days of America survives in the form of a great love for the outdoors. The ideal of the 'backwoodsman' who could build a cabin like Willy and live in harmony with the land like Biff was a popular one, and this ideal seems to be welcome in the play, although it does not satisfy Willy. Willy talks of competitiveness, and this is also an essential element of the masculine attitude that underlies capitalism. It is necessary to beat the opposition at all costs if you are to succeed, and Happy shows he is capable of this, even though he acknowledges that it

CHECK THE BOOK

Contemporary documents about the American Dream are reproduced in *Understanding Death of a Salesman: A Student Casebook* by Brenda Murphy and Susan C. W. Abbotson (1999).

makes him inhuman. Happy competes sexually because he cannot compete on a work basis with the executives.

McCARTHYISM

The anti-Communist hysteria of the McCarthyite period was inescapable, since Communism was seen as a threat to the American way of life. Public figures were arraigned by Senator Joseph McCarthy and asked to prove that they had not been Communist sympathisers. This was a hysterical reaction to the Cold War between America and Russia when America feared any left-wing ideology. Many writers took advertisements in the theatrical trade press attacking the Communists, and Arthur Miller was asked by Columbia Pictures to do this before Stanley Kramer's film of *Death of Salesman* was released. Miller refused. Columbia resorted to making a short film at a university business school which consisted of interviews with business professors, who patiently explained that Willy Loman was not a typical salesman and that selling was an honourable profession. Miller was forced to accept this indignity. This surprising fact shows how deeply Arthur Miller's play had penetrated the American mind. Nowadays, of course, attacking consumerism is not at all unusual. Arthur Miller, however, has said that 'the social drama is to me only incidentally an arraignment of society' (original edition of *A View From the Bridge*). It would be wrong to think that the purpose of the play was to blame society alone. The point of the play is not that the economic system does not work, but that its ideology distorts man's true nature. In the America of 1949, this was seen by many as a dangerous slur on the ordinary American.

CHECK THE FILM
Stanley Kramer's film was released in 1951 and starred Fredric March as Willy.

LITERARY BACKGROUND

In his early work, Arthur Miller adopted the **realist** mode and, in keeping with **naturalism**, also specified exactly which props were to be on stage. The early love for realism was bred at university, where he encountered nineteenth-century writers such as Henrik Ibsen. *All My Sons*, for example, was a piece of conventional realism. In *Death of a Salesman*, the historical details are accurate, and the language is taken directly from American life. Arthur Miller has said, in his introduction to his *Collected Plays* (reprinted in

CHECK THE NET
See http://www.
teachervision.com/
lesson-plans/lesson-
3499.html for a
collection of wide-
ranging questions
and assignments on
the play and its
contemporary
setting.

Plays: One, p. 52): 'I have stood squarely in conventional realism; I have tried to expand it with an imposition of various forms in order to speak more directly, even more abruptly and nakedly of what has moved me behind the visible façades of life.' Miller feels that realism as a style can become confining and inhibit the playwright from giving us the real 'forces and values' which lie behind appearances. If the play has to be realistic throughout, then we can never, for example, see into the mind of the main character, since this is not possible in our usual lives. In *Death of a Salesman*, therefore, Arthur Miller adds **Expressionism** to social realism to overcome this difficulty. Bertolt Brecht argued that realism was drama which revealed 'society's causal network', the interplay of forces that actually drive us to act in certain ways. The ultimate meaning of theatrical realism is not that what happens on stage is what happens in real life, but that we believe that we have seen the characters driven by credible motives and pressures.

A classic American Expressionist play is Elmer Rice's *The Adding Machine* (1923) in which a revolving stage was used to create a 'flashback' effect as in films. In this play, realism is abandoned in order to make visible on stage the kinds of mental events which can only be reproduced through symbols. The play attempts to express the dehumanising effect of a mass society where individuals feel as if they are no more than parts of a machine. It is about a man who, after working as a bookkeeper for many years, is replaced by an adding machine. In response to the sacking, the stage revolves and the music grows louder until there is only a massive din. We are made to experience dehumanisation as if we too were suffering it. It is also generally recognised that Clifford Odets's play *Awake and Sing!* (1935), which includes a suicide by an old man to enable insurance to be passed on, was an inspiration for Arthur Miller. Eugene O'Neill's *The Iceman Cometh* (1946), which also concerns a salesman, was another source of inspiration.

Arthur Miller has had a great influence on contemporary American playwrights of a younger generation such as David Mamet, whose play *Glengarry Glen Ross* (1983), about salesmen in an estate agency, acknowledges a debt to Miller and this particular play.

In *Death of a Salesman* we see an element of Expressionism when Willy goes to ask Howard for a non-travelling sales job. The machine that Howard wheels on is an early sound-recording device, and it has captured the sounds of Howard's children learning historical facts by rote. It is clearly an echo of the Expressionist form which attempted to project the mind of the main character onto the stage using large, unusual symbols rather than real things. The sound-recording machine brings back the past truthfully and when Willy bumps against it accidentally, it makes an ugly and unbearable noise that has to be stifled quickly. Willy does not want to hear the sounds of a happy family or to feel that the past can be captured for ever.

Expressionist theatre is a cry of despair on the part of an alienated individual, and Arthur Miller merges this expertly with realism. Miller had originally intended to call the play *The Inside of His Head*, which would have clearly linked it with Expressionism. Some psychoanalysts have linked Willy's scenes from the past with the brain's desire to keep back memories that are too painful to consider again. This is known in psychoanalytic terms as 'the return of the repressed', since psychoanalysts believe that any repressed emotion will eventually reappear, albeit in another form. Willy's forbidden thoughts, such as the memory of his affair, recur at crucial moments and often show a contrasting side of his personality to that which he is presenting to the world.

CHECK THE BOOK

In *Modern Drama in Theory and Practice: Expressionism and Epic Theatre*, vol. 3 (1981), J. L. Styan describes the play as 'a conventional two-act play, but so broken into episodic fragments by lighting and spatial changes that it conveyed the free association of the mind'.

World events	Arthur Miller	Literary context
	1944 *The Story of GI Joe,* a screenplay, is written *The Man Who Had All the Luck* is staged	**1944** *Antigone* by French playwright Jean Anouilh is staged *Huis clos* (*In Camera*) by French playwright Jean-Paul Sartre is staged Tennessee Williams's *The Glass Menagerie* is staged
1945 Franklin D. Roosevelt dies; he is succeeded as US president by Harry S. Truman The Second World War ends	**1945** *Focus,* a novel, is published	
1946 Winston Churchill coins the term 'Iron Curtain'		**1946** J. B. Priestley's *An Inspector Calls* is staged Eugene O'Neill's *The Iceman Cometh* is staged Terence Rattigan's *The Winslow Boy* is staged
1947 US foreign policy aims to restrict the expansion of Communism	**1947** *All My Sons* is staged	**1947** Tennessee Williams's *A Streetcar Named Desire* is staged J. B. Priestley's *The Linden Tree* is staged
1948 Communist coup in Czechoslovakia		**1948** Terence Rattigan's *The Browning Version* is staged
1949 North Atlantic Treaty is signed by Western states	**1949** *Death of a Salesman* is staged, and wins the Pulitzer Prize	**1949** T. S. Eliot's *The Cocktail Party* is staged Bertolt Brecht's *Mutter Courage* (*Mother Courage*) is staged
1950 Senator McCarthy claims the US State Department is full of Communists, and heads an enquiry into 'un-American activities' that lasts until 1954	**1950** Arthur Miller's adaptation of Henrik Ibsen's play, *An Enemy of the People,* is staged	**1950** Terence Rattigan's *Who is Sylvia?* is staged *La Cantatrice chauve* (*The Bald Prima Donna*) by playwright Eugène Ionesco is staged

World events	Arthur Miller	Literary context
1951 British diplomats Guy Burgess and Donald Maclean defect to the USSR		**1951** Christopher Fry's *A Sleep of Prisoners* is staged
1952 George VI of England dies		**1952** Agatha Christie's *The Mousetrap* is staged Terence Rattigan's *The Deep Blue Sea* is staged *En attendant Godot*, the French version of *Waiting for Godot* by Samuel Beckett, is staged
1953 Joseph Stalin dies; he is succeeded as Communist Party secretary by Nikita Khrushchev Coronation of Elizabeth II in England	**1953** *The Crucible* is staged	**1953** Tennessee Williams's *Camino Real* is staged
1954 US hydrogen bomb is tested at Bikini atoll	**1954** Miller is denied a passport to visit Brussels for the European première of *The Crucible* on the grounds of it not being in the best interest of the country	**1954** *Under Milk Wood* by Dylan Thomas is broadcast on British radio Terence Rattigan's *Separate Tables* is staged
1955 The Warsaw Pact, an Eastern European defence treaty, is signed by Communist nations	**1955** *A View from the Bridge* is staged *A Memory of Two Mondays* is staged Miller divorces his first wife, Mary Slattery	**1955** Samuel Beckett's *Waiting for Godot* is staged in English Tennessee Williams's *Cat on a Hot Tin Roof* is staged
	1956 Miller marries Marilyn Monroe	

Some of the following titles are now out of print; these books are often available in school or college libraries.

Gayle Austin, *Feminist Theories for Dramatic Criticism*, University of Michigan Press, 1990
Contains an essay on *Death of a Salesman* which uses Eve Kosofsky Sedgwick's theories of homosexual exchange and compares the text with Lillian Hellman's *Another Part of the Forest*

C. W. E. Bigsby, *A Critical Introduction to Twentieth-Century American Drama*, vol. 3: *Beyond Broadway*, Cambridge University Press, 1985

C. W. E. Bigsby, *File on Miller*, Methuen, 1987
A potted version of each of Arthur Miller's plays with details of performances plus selected quotations on matters of major interest

C. W. E. Bigsby, *Arthur Miller and Company*, Methuen, 1990
A collection of conversations with actors who have been involved in the work

Harold Bloom (ed.), *Willy Loman*, Chelsea House, 1990
Bloom attacks Arthur Miller's identification of Willy and King Lear as overstated and argues for an interpretation in terms of the Jewish family. In the same collection, Kay Stanton describes the play as a 'male-oriented version of the American Dream'

Harold Bloom (ed.), *Arthur Miller's Death of a Salesman*, Contemporary Literary Views, Chelsea House, 1995

John Russell Brown and Bernard Harris (eds.), *American Theatre*, Edward Arnold, 1967
See the essay about the Liberal notion of the free individual by Eric Mottram entitled 'Arthur Miller: The Development of a Political Dramatist in America'

Gerald M. Burkowitz, *American Drama of the Twentieth Century*, Longman, 1992

Neil Carson, *Arthur Miller*, Macmillan, 1982
A brief essay on this play is contained in a survey of all Arthur Miller's work. This focuses in particular on the father-son relationship and Willy's inability to imitate his own father

Larry W. Cook, 'The Function of Ben and Dave Singleman in *Death of a Salesman*', *Notes on Contemporary Literature V*, January 1975, pp. 7–9

Robert W. Corrigan (ed.), *Arthur Miller: A Collection of Critical Essays*, Prentice-Hall, 1969
This very useful collection contains essays by Eric Mottram and Raymond Williams on Arthur Miller in general

Bernard F. Dukore, *Death of a Salesman and The Crucible: Text and Performance*, Macmillan, 1989
> A brief survey of the major theoretical debates and some useful information on the famous performances of the play

Anthony Easthope, *What a Man's Gotta Do: The Masculine Myth in Popular Culture*, Paladin, 1986

Martin Esslin, *The Field of Drama: How the Signs of Drama Create Meaning on Stage and Screen*, Methuen, 1987
> A very good introduction to the ways in which drama in general can be interpreted

Leah Hadomi, 'Fantasy and Reality: Dramatic Rhythm in *Death of a Salesman*', *Modern Drama*, 1988, pp. 157–74
> A structuralist approach which sees the play as setting a tension between opposites, mainly dream and reality

Karl Harshbarger, *The Burning Jungle: An Analysis of Miller's 'Death of a Salesman'*, University Press of America, 1978

Ronald Hayman, *Arthur Miller*, Heinemann, 1970
> A eulogy of Arthur Miller and a focus on the notion of salesmanship and the extent to which this concept has infiltrated Willy's personal relationships

Ronald Hayman, *How to Read a Play*, Grove Press, revised and updated 1999

Esther M. Jackson, '*Death of a Salesman*: Tragic Myth in the Modern Theater', *College Language Association Journal VII*, September 1963, pp. 63–76

Stephen A. Marino (ed.), *The Salesman Has a Birthday*, University Press of America, 2000
> A collection of essays from the fifth international Arthur Miller conference, celebrating fifty years since the first performance

Stephen A. Marino and Francis Oakley, *A Language Study of Arthur Miller's Plays: The Plays in the Colloquial*, Studies in American Literature, vol. 53, Edwin Mellen Press, 2002

Robert A. Martin (ed.), *The Theater Essays of Arthur Miller*, Da Capo Press, New York, 1986

Arthur Miller, *Salesman in Beijing*, Methuen, 1983
> An account of staging the play in China

FURTHER READING

Arthur Miller, *Timebends: A Life*, Methuen, 1987

Arthur Miller, *Plays: One*, Methuen, 1988
    The introduction, orginally written by Arthur miller for his *Collected Plays* in 1958, is an indispensable guide to his views on the play

Arthur Miller, *On Politics and the Art of Acting*, Viking Press, 2001

Brenda Murphy, *Miller: Death of a Salesman* (Plays in Production), Cambridge University Press, 1995
    A useful account of the performance history of the play

Brenda Murphy and Susan C. W. Abbotson, *Understanding Death of a Salesman: A Student Casebook to Issues, Sources and Historical Documents*, Greenwood Press, 1999

John Orr and Dragan Klaic (eds.), *Terrorism and Modern Drama*, Edinburgh University Press, 1990
    Contains an interesting essay by Lado Kralj on 'Individualist and Collectivist Models of Terror in German Expressionist Drama', which examines aspects of **Expressionism** which can be found in Arthur Miller's play

Matthew C. Roudané (ed.), *Approaches to Teaching Miller's Death of a Salesman* (Approaches to Teaching World Literature Series, 52), Modern Language Association of America, 1995

David Savran, *Communists, Cowboys and Queers: The Politics of Masculinity in the Work of Arthur Miller and Tennessee Williams*, University of Minnesota Press, 1992
    Touches lightly on Arthur Miller's play and its avoidance of homosexuality

R. Selden, *Practising Theory and Reading Literature: An Introduction*, Harvester Wheatsheaf, 1989
    In Chapter 7, 'Binary Oppositions: Arthur Miller', Selden demonstrates the application of structuralist technique to the play by showing how certain repeated sets of opposites occur and how these are related to themes such as morality

Thomas Siebold (ed.), *Readings on Death of a Salesman*, Greenhaven Press, 1998

George Steiner, *Death of Tragedy*, Faber, 1961, revised edition 1975

J. L. Styan, *Modern Drama in Theory and Practice: Expressionism and Epic Theatre*, vol. 3, Cambridge University Press, 1981

> A very useful guide to the Expressionist tendency worldwide with a brief examination of how *Death of A Salesman* fits into this tradition

Gerald Weales (ed.), *Death of a Salesman: Text and Criticism*, Viking Critical Library, Penguin USA, 1996

Dennis Welland, *Miller: The Playwright*, Methuen, 1979; revised edition 1983

> Treats the whole oeuvre, but takes an interesting critical approach to *Death of a Salesman*. The argument is that Linda acts as a mouthpiece for Arthur Miller, but that she is 'too good for the play' and that her characterisation therefore fails

Raymond Williams, *Drama from Ibsen to Brecht*, Penguin, 1968

AUDIO TAPES

Death of a Salesman by Arthur Miller is published by Harper Audio

VIDEO

Death of a Salesman, 1985

> Starring Dustin Hoffman and John Malkovich, directed by Volker Schlöndorff

CD-ROM

Mary B. Collins, *Death of a Salesman: A Unit Plan*, Teacher's Pet Publications, 2000

> Lesson plans for teaching the play

catharsis the emotional relief that results from a tragic drama which inspires fear and pity in the onlooker

Expressionism a European artistic movement that started *c.*1900 in Germany as a revolt against **realism**. Instead of attempting to represent the world conventionally and objectively, Expressionist writers show reality distorted by an emotional or abnormal state of mind, even by madness

hamartia the error of judgement which a tragic hero makes and which leads to the hero's downfall

metaphor describing one thing as being another

naturalism a mode of **realism** based on the faithful and detailed copying of nature, with no attempt to improve or idealise the subject

paradigm a perfect example of something, as used for the purposes of illustration

realism writing that seeks to portray an accurate account of the way that society works

AUTHOR OF THESE NOTES

Adrian Page has taught literature and drama at degree level and is now a principal lecturer in Media Arts at the University of Luton. He has published on literary theory and semiotics and he is the editor of *The Death of the Playwright? Modern British Drama and Literary Theory* (Macmillan, 1992).

General editors

Martin Gray, former Head of the Department of English Studies at the University of Stirling, and of Literary Studies at the University of Luton

Professor A. N. Jeffares, Emeritus Professor of English, University of Stirling

Maya Angelou
I Know Why the Caged Bird Sings

Jane Austen
Pride and Prejudice

Alan Ayckbourn
Absent Friends

Elizabeth Barrett Browning
Selected Poems

Robert Bolt
A Man for All Seasons

Harold Brighouse
Hobson's Choice

Charlotte Brontë
Jane Eyre

Emily Brontë
Wuthering Heights

Shelagh Delaney
A Taste of Honey

Charles Dickens
David Copperfield
Great Expectations
Hard Times
Oliver Twist

Roddy Doyle
Paddy Clarke Ha Ha Ha

George Eliot
Silas Marner
The Mill on the Floss

Anne Frank
The Diary of a Young Girl

William Golding
Lord of the Flies

Oliver Goldsmith
She Stoops to Conquer

Willis Hall
The Long and the Short and the Tall

Thomas Hardy
Far from the Madding Crowd
The Mayor of Casterbridge
Tess of the d'Urbervilles
The Withered Arm and other Wessex Tales

L.P. Hartley
The Go-Between

Seamus Heaney
Selected Poems

Susan Hill
I'm the King of the Castle

Barry Hines
A Kestrel for a Knave

Louise Lawrence
Children of the Dust

Harper Lee
To Kill a Mockingbird

Laurie Lee
Cider with Rosie

Arthur Miller
The Crucible
A View from the Bridge

Robert O'Brien
Z for Zachariah

Frank O'Connor
My Oedipus Complex and Other Stories

George Orwell
Animal Farm

J.B. Priestley
An Inspector Calls
When We Are Married

Willy Russell
Educating Rita
Our Day Out

J.D. Salinger
The Catcher in the Rye

William Shakespeare
Henry IV Part I
Henry V
Julius Caesar
Macbeth
The Merchant of Venice
A Midsummer Night's Dream
Much Ado About Nothing
Romeo and Juliet
The Tempest
Twelfth Night

George Bernard Shaw
Pygmalion

Mary Shelley
Frankenstein

R.C. Sherriff
Journey's End

Rukshana Smith
Salt on the snow

John Steinbeck
Of Mice and Men

Robert Louis Stevenson
Dr Jekyll and Mr Hyde

Jonathan Swift
Gulliver's Travels

Robert Swindells
Daz 4 Zoe

Mildred D. Taylor
Roll of Thunder, Hear My Cry

Mark Twain
Huckleberry Finn

James Watson
Talking in Whispers

Edith Wharton
Ethan Frome

William Wordsworth
Selected Poems

A Choice of Poets

Mystery Stories of the Nineteenth Century including The Signalman

Nineteenth Century Short Stories

Poetry of the First World War

Six Women Poets

For the AQA Anthology:

Duffy and Armitage & Pre-1914 Poetry

Heaney and Clarke & Pre-1914 Poetry

Poems from Different Cultures

Margaret Atwood
Cat's Eye
The Handmaid's Tale

Jane Austen
Emma
Mansfield Park
Persuasion
Pride and Prejudice
Sense and Sensibility

Alan Bennett
Talking Heads

William Blake
Songs of Innocence and of Experience

Charlotte Brontë
Jane Eyre
Villette

Emily Brontë
Wuthering Heights

Angela Carter
Nights at the Circus

Geoffrey Chaucer
The Franklin's Prologue and Tale
The Merchant's Prologue and Tale
The Miller's Prologue and Tale
The Prologue to the Canterbury Tales
The Wife of Bath's Prologue and Tale

Samuel Coleridge
Selected Poems

Joseph Conrad
Heart of Darkness

Daniel Defoe
Moll Flanders

Charles Dickens
Bleak House
Great Expectations
Hard Times

Emily Dickinson
Selected Poems

John Donne
Selected Poems

Carol Ann Duffy
Selected Poems

George Eliot
Middlemarch
The Mill on the Floss

T.S. Eliot
Selected Poems
The Waste Land

F. Scott Fitzgerald
The Great Gatsby

E.M. Forster
A Passage to India

Brian Friel
Translations

Thomas Hardy
Jude the Obscure
The Mayor of Casterbridge
The Return of the Native
Selected Poems
Tess of the d'Urbervilles

Seamus Heaney
Selected Poems from 'Opened Ground'

Nathaniel Hawthorne
The Scarlet Letter

Homer
The Iliad
The Odyssey

Aldous Huxley
Brave New World

Kazuo Ishiguro
The Remains of the Day

Ben Jonson
The Alchemist

James Joyce
Dubliners

John Keats
Selected Poems

Philip Larkin
The Whitsun Weddings and Selected Poems

Christopher Marlowe
Doctor Faustus
Edward II

Arthur Miller
Death of a Salesman

John Milton
Paradise Lost Books I & II

Toni Morrison
Beloved

George Orwell
Nineteen Eighty-Four

Sylvia Plath
Selected Poems

Alexander Pope
Rape of the Lock & Selected Poems

William Shakespeare
Antony and Cleopatra
As You Like It
Hamlet
Henry IV Part I
King Lear
Macbeth
Measure for Measure
The Merchant of Venice
A Midsummer Night's Dream
Much Ado About Nothing
Othello
Richard II
Richard III
Romeo and Juliet
The Taming of the Shrew
The Tempest
Twelfth Night
The Winter's Tale

George Bernard Shaw
Saint Joan

Mary Shelley
Frankenstein

Jonathan Swift
Gulliver's Travels and A Modest Proposal

Alfred Tennyson
Selected Poems

Virgil
The Aeneid

Alice Walker
The Color Purple

Oscar Wilde
The Importance of Being Earnest

Tennessee Williams
A Streetcar Named Desire
The Glass Menagerie

Jeanette Winterson
Oranges Are Not the Only Fruit

John Webster
The Duchess of Malfi

Virginia Woolf
To the Lighthouse

William Wordsworth
The Prelude and Selected Poems

W.B. Yeats
Selected Poems

Metaphysical Poets

THE ULTIMATE WEB SITE FOR THE ULTIMATE LITERATURE GUIDES

At York Notes we believe in helping you achieve exam success. Log on to **www.yorknotes.com** and see how we have made revision even easier, with over 300 titles available to download twenty-four hours a day. The downloads have lots of additional features such as pop-up boxes providing instant glossary definitions, user-friendly links to every part of the guide, and scanned illustrations offering visual appeal. All you need to do is log on to **www.yorknotes.com** and download the books you need to help you achieve exam success.

KEY FEATURES:

Details on how York Notes can help you

Menu Bar to help you find your way around the site

Details on how to download York Notes

Quick Search facility to help you find the titles you need

Link to news about new titles

List of top-selling downloads